More Praise for *The Best Teacher in You*

"The very best teachers are the ones who know their learning is never done. Bringing together the expertise of academic research, this book offers tangible ways that reflective, growth-oriented teachers at any level can help themselves continue to grow their practice."
—Ellen Moir, CEO, New Teacher Center

"This is highly practical, with real classroom case examples, useful tools, well-grounded guiding principles, and more. It is honest and intensely relevant for the teachers and the schools that are under undue pressures these days, a book that has heart and soul."
—Jim Evers, retired teacher and author of *Becoming a School Where Everyone Matters* and *Crisis in School Management*

"The authors have uncovered insights that characterize the extraordinary teach-ers who produce results three or four times higher than normal teachers. Their careful insight and compelling illustrations provide guidance that every teacher, parent, and leader will find useful."
—Kim Cameron, Associate Dean and William Russell Kelly Professor of Management and Organizations, Ross School of Business, and Professor of Higher Education, School of Education, University of Michigan

"This book identifies the characteristics of teachers who really make a difference. The highly effective teacher will feel reinforced. The teacher looking to improve will learn from stories and research that are inspirational and implementable. This should be required reading for everyone entering the education profession."
—R. Kirk Hamilton, PhD, Executive Director, Buckeye Association of School Administrators

"In the same way transformational leaders make a difference in the lives of their employees, transformational teachers inspire students to exceed expectations. Based on the authors' groundbreaking research, this book is for anyone interested in helping students reach their highest potential."
—Julian Barling, PhD, Borden Chair of Leadership, Queen's School of Business, and author of *The Science of Leadership*

"Teaching is more than pedagogical technique or student test scores. The authors capture the complexity of teaching and provide a road map for understanding the dynamics of what it truly means to be a highly effective teacher."
—Thomas J. Lasley, Executive Director, Learn to Earn Dayton, Dayton Foundation, and Professor, School of Education and Health Sciences, University of Dayton

"Can highly effective teachers help their peers 'set classrooms on fire'? *The Best Teacher in You* not only says yes but also tells us how. Teachers, parents, and public-policy makers should take this insightful and inspiring study to heart."
—Richard Celeste, former President, Colorado College, and 64th Governor of Ohio

"This book is a wonderful text for a professional development session with teachers who have been in the field a few years and were feeling as if they were not getting the most out of their students."

—**Dr. Joy Cowdery, Janet Brown Rothwell Distinguished Professor of Education, Muskingum University Education Department**

"*The Best Teacher in You* is an affirming and encouraging resource, challenging teachers at all stages of their careers to reflect on their practices and continue growing and developing as teachers and learners."

—**Tricia Ebner, NBCT, gifted intervention specialist and member, Ohio Educator Leader Cadre, Lake Middle School**

"*The Best Teacher in You* provides real-world examples and practical tools to help teachers be the best teacher they can be for their students. The book provides practical and insightful examples from some of the best educators identified through a rich, data-driven analysis of actual student performance."

—**Larry Hilsheimer, Executive Vice President and Chief Financial Officer, Scotts Miracle-Gro**

"There are multiple paths to uncover the best teacher within. *The Best Teacher in You* introduces a framework that explores effective, powerful practices to leverage individual educators' strengths and empower them despite the challenges of society."

—**Richard Lewis, Executive Director, Ohio School Boards Association**

"This book provides powerful insights into highly effective teachers and the symbiotic relationships they foster with their students that yield improved teaching and learning for all. The stories are inspirational, and the authors do an amazing job of providing practical strategies that can lead to the transformation of the practice by others."

—**Julie Baker Finck, PhD, President, Barbara Bush Houston Literacy Foundation**

"Better schools with better outcomes result from the *best* teachers. This book dissects the attitudes, behaviors, challenges, and personal philosophies that drive highly effective teachers."

—**Michael Gonsiorowski, Regional President, PNC Bank**

"*The Best Teacher in You* moves us past the histrionics of value-added measures by using them to actually identify great teachers. Following up the statistical evidence with deep qualitative research, this book seeks to find out what makes great teachers tick. This important work is an affirmation that foundational elements like quality relationships, a growth mindset, a supportive environment, and high expectations are what matter most in education."

—**Jason Glass, Superintendent and Chief Learner, Eagle County Schools**

"For the highly effective teacher that seems to be locked up inside and is yearning to get out, *The Best Teacher in You* is the key to opening the door."

—**Carl F. Kohrt, PhD, President and CEO (retired), Battelle Memorial Institute**

The
Best Teacher
in **You**

The
Best Teacher
in You

*How to Accelerate Learning
and Change Lives*

Robert E. Quinn

Katherine Heynoski

Mike Thomas

Gretchen M. Spreitzer

BK

Berrett–Koehler Publishers, Inc.
San Francisco
a BK Life book

Berrett-Koehler Publishers, Inc.
235 Montgomery Street, Suite 650, San Francisco, CA 94104-2916
Tel: (415) 288-0260   Fax: (415) 362-2512   www.bkconnection.com

Ordering Information

Quantity sales. Special discounts are available on quantity purchases by corporations,
associations, and others. For details, contact the "Special Sales Department" at the
Berrett-Koehler address above.

Individual sales. Berrett-Koehler publications are available through most bookstores.
They can also be ordered directly from Berrett-Koehler:
Tel: (800) 929-2929; Fax: (802) 864-7626; www.bkconnection.com.
Orders for college textbook/course adoption use. Please contact Berrett-Koehler:
Tel: (800) 929-2929; Fax: (802) 864-7626.
Orders by U.S. trade bookstores and wholesalers. Please contact Ingram Publisher
Services, Tel: (800) 509-4887; Fax: (800) 838-1149; E-mail: customer.service@
ingrampublisherservices.com; or visit www.ingrampublisherservices.com/Ordering
for details about electronic ordering.

Berrett-Koehler and the BK logo are registered trademarks of
Berrett-Koehler Publishers, Inc.

Printed in the United States of America

Berrett-Koehler books are printed on long-lasting acid-free paper. When it is available, we choose paper that has been manufactured by environmentally responsible
processes. These may include using trees grown in sustainable forests, incorporating
recycled paper, minimizing chlorine in bleaching, or recycling the energy produced
at the paper mill.

Cataloging data is available from the Library of Congress, catalog no. 2014008286.

ISBN 978-1-62656-178-6

18   17   16   15   14   10   9   8   7   6   5   4   3   2   1

Cover design by Cassandra Chu.
Interior design and composition by Gary Palmatier, Ideas to Images. Elizabeth
von Radics, copyeditor; Mike Mollett, proofreader; Alexandra Nickerson, indexer.

To all the teachers who make a difference in the lives of their students—and in particular the special teachers in our own lives who planted the seeds for this book.

Contents

Learning from Highly Effective Teachers

The creation of a thousand forests is in one acorn.

—Ralph Waldo Emerson
Essays: First Series

I N MOST SYSTEMS THERE ARE ONE OR MORE POSITIVE OUTLIERS—PEOPLE who are subject to the same constraints as others but who exceed expectations. This means that they, in some way, think and behave differently. Their thinking is somehow more complex than conventional thinking, their behavior is somehow more adaptive than conventional behaviors, and their outcomes are more generative than conventional outcomes. Some of these people work in our public schools. They are highly effective teachers who accelerate learning and change lives.

Exceeding Expectations

In recent years our education system has been under great pressure. There have been calls for expanded accountability, particularly through standardized testing and more-rigorous teacher evaluation processes. Attention has been turned to the use of value-added scores to assess how much student progress a given teacher stimulates. These scores have been at the center of much controversy. In this book we use them in a different way.

Over the past seven years, we have worked closely with teachers across Ohio, Tennessee, and Texas who consistently achieved high value-added scores. These are teachers who, by objective measures, produce more than expected learning year in and year out. In this book we do not advance a position on value-added scores. We only use them to help identify the highly effective teachers (HETs) profiled in this book. (If you want to learn more, we provide some background on value-added scores in the research box below.)

We brought HETs into workshops to help them learn from each other so that they could become even more effective. At these workshops HETs spent a day interviewing one another, sharing their assumptions, and telling stories about their practice.

In addition to the workshops, which involved more than 350 HETs, we have also held intensive interviews with 30 of the highest-performing teachers in the state of Ohio. These teachers were at the very top of the value-added scale in three of the previous four years. In this book you will meet these teachers and read their stories. (In those stories all student names have been changed.)

Their accounts may sometimes surprise you and cause you to think about teaching and learning in a more complex and adaptive way. That is what their stories forced us to do. Throughout this book we reflect on their experiences and offer some tools to help you assess and grow your own practice. Our hope is that the tools will help you liberate the best teacher in you again and again.

RESEARCH FOUNDATIONS

Value-Added Scores

Value-added is a phrase that has become prominent in recent years. The term is associated with the effort to objectively measure teacher effectiveness. A classroom-level value-added score is a quantitative assessment of how much a teacher contributes to student learning in one academic year. It measures the change in the standardized test scores of students in a given class, or in multiple classes, taught by a given teacher. The scores are adjusted for differences in student characteristics and student scores on previous tests. The standard for academic growth in most states is the amount of academic growth students experience in a typical classroom.

Value-added scores at the top of the scale seem to be an indicator of powerful classroom dynamics. A large-scale study of the relationship between value-added scores and student outcomes examined the records of 1 million children who progressed from fourth grade to adulthood.[1] The results were impressive. The students of HETs are more likely to attend college, earn higher salaries, live in better neighborhoods, and save more, and they are less likely to experience teenage pregnancy. The three economists who published the study were initially skeptical of value-added scores, but they concluded that "great teachers create great value." In the paper the authors make some policy suggestions that have stirred great controversy, but the findings appear to remain valid.

Value-added scores are not without controversy. Standardized test scores do not always reliably measure student achievement, and a single measure cannot fully capture everything teachers contribute to student learning. Initially, we had our own reservations about the validity of value-added data, but our interactions with HETs convinced us that high value-added scores are associated with more than just an increase in test scores. We also contacted a number of principals and asked them to tell us about teachers in their building who consistently had high value-added scores. Almost every response was some variation of the statement *He or she is one of the best teachers in my school.*

Who Should Read This Book?

This book is written for teachers at all levels and in any field who are hungry to learn and develop. Experienced teachers who currently excel may find companionship in this book. In our workshops and interviews, we found that most schools are uncomfortable with the "highly effective" distinction. We heard many stories of principals telling teachers to keep quiet about being invited to these workshops. But when we brought these teachers together, they were thrilled to hear from one another. This book may provide companionship and learning for those who feel that their excellence goes unseen.

Experienced teachers who feel discouraged may find inspiration in this book. The stories of HETs are of developing teachers who learn to move to higher levels of performance. Their accounts may stimulate the courage to engage in new experiments and new learning.

Current students in teacher education programs and new teachers may find higher levels of aspiration in this book. The performance achieved by HETs illustrates excellence and suggests paths to get there. The accounts of the HETs may bring an expanded vision of what is possible.

Administrators and policy makers may find a new strategic perspective. The administrative world is dominated by a problem-solving perspective. Policies are shaped to fix what is wrong with the system. HETs illustrate what is most right with the system. The excellence of HETs invites a shift in focus from what should be fixed to what should be pursued. Seeking out, paying attention to, and learning from the best teachers may have a payoff. This book may instill a desire for such a shift in perspective.

People responsible for the professional development of educators may find a new approach to their work. When we present the material in this book, people often ask, "Can HETs be developed?" We respond that teachers are more likely to become HETs if they are challenged and supported in the same ways that HETs challenge and support their students. That is, if we were to teach teachers the way the best teachers teach students, teacher development might accelerate and lives might change.

There is a large group of people outside professional education who desire to become more effective. These people may find that teaching is simply a metaphor for leading and that great teaching is a metaphor for great leading. By reading about the work of HETs, it may be possible to gain insights into how to better accelerate learning and change lives in any setting.

While this book is intended to help practitioners reflect on their own experiences, scholars may find some insights worthy of attention.

In this work we do not make systematic comparisons between HETs and other teachers, so we can draw no generalizable conclusions about what differentiates them. We do however make comparisons. As students, each of the authors spent thousands of hours in classrooms. We then became professional educators. As a result, we made many observations about teaching and formed assumptions about what makes teaching more or less effective. As we listened to the HETs, we compared what they said with our own accumulated experiences. We particularly focused on the things that challenged and surprised us. Their statements may also surprise you.

In each chapter we offer a case study, and then we make sense of the processes being described. From our qualitative data, we provide insights and offer propositions about effective teaching. Until these are systematically tested, we will not know if they hold. We hope that the grounded observations made here might stimulate such work.

How to Read This Book

Over the course of this book, we embrace the metaphor of a growing tree. From the visual on the cover to the images that are interspersed throughout, you will find the unfolding tree—from seed to seedling to mature tree. We believe it to be an apt metaphor for the unfolding and the development of the very best teachers.

A tree begins its development by shedding the husk that surrounds the living seed. As the husk is shed, the tree begins to grow in two directions simultaneously: upward to produce a seedling and downward to produce a strong and widespread root system. Roots serve several important functions for the growth of the tree, including stabilizing and anchoring it to withstand weather of all kinds and nourishing it with water and other nutrients in the soil. It is also interesting that roots do not grow haphazardly; they constantly grow toward higher concentrations of the water and the nutrients that the tree needs to grow.

Above the ground the tree grows many branches that reach toward the sky. Branches support leaves that produce the energy the tree needs to survive. Each branch is autonomous: if it fails or breaks, other branches can still grow and thrive. Great teachers grow in similar ways. They experiment, they extend themselves, and they find new ways to nourish themselves; realizing that not all ideas are viable but with many new ideas percolating, teachers can continue to develop themselves and their students in a dance of continuous learning.

Throughout the book we also include the following symbols that use the tree metaphor to highlight the different elements to which we want to draw your attention:

 The sprouting acorn icon identifies an overview of the content of the current chapter.

 The roots icon provides the research foundation behind the ideas being shared.

 The leaf icon calls attention to practical teaching tips from the teacher who is profiled in each chapter.

 The acorn icon indicates the idea of planting seeds. We offer questions to help you more deeply reflect on the key points in each chapter as it relates to your own teaching practice.

 Finally, the tree icon indicates a call to action, where you can get ideas to grow your practice.

Each chapter is built around the story of one extraordinary teacher and how he or she has developed (through successes and failures) to have a positive impact on students. We identify powerful practices that serve to accelerate and deepen the learning of students as well as the teacher. Through the inspiration of these extraordinary models, we share a message that makes it possible for all teachers to start their own journey toward excellence.

The book is built around something we call the BFK•Connect Framework (see inside front cover for a color illustration), a model that establishes four core dimensions of educator effectiveness. Later chapters examine how powerful transformation comes from transcending the individual aspects of each of the four dimensions to build higher-level capacities, including co-creation with students, empowerment, and transformational leadership in the classroom.

Structure of the Book

Chapter 1 presents two views of education. The first is directive and is based on the assumption that education is a hierarchical process of knowledge transfer. Most of us are already familiar with the directive perspective because it is the model that many of us experienced as we grew up. The second view of education is based on an assumption of transformational growth through co-creation. It suggests that education is an organic, adaptive process of knowledge creation. The second perspective does not deny or negate the first. The need for the directive perspective never goes away. The co-creative perspective includes and enlarges the first, making it possible to both broaden and deepen learning.

Chapter 2 proposes that a person must transcend conventional assumptions and operate from an expanded set of beliefs to obtain extraordinary outcomes. Those beliefs may, by conventional standards, seem almost paradoxical. The chapter introduces the BFK•Connect Framework for thinking about how differences can be connected and become mutually reinforcing. It suggests that performance increases as we learn to adapt and that as we learn to adapt we become more complex, that is, more able to see differences and integrate them in generative ways.

Chapters 3 and 4 reflect on how to leverage our strengths without being limited by them. Building on our strengths while recognizing their limitations helps us leave our comfort zone, have new experiences that challenge our working assumptions, and move toward excellence. Each teacher's developmental path is unique, but the journey is facilitated by understanding the framework introduced in chapter 2 and elaborated on in chapters 3 and 4.

Chapter 5 explores how teachers can empower themselves despite the challenges they face. HETs claim to experience the same barriers and feel the same frustrations as their peers, but they seem to respond with unusual resilience. Rather than focus on the barriers, they tend to focus on their higher purpose and they keep learning. That purpose is to liberate the potential that already exists in students. One aspect of this strategy is to model the change they wish to see in their students.

Chapter 6 examines the empowerment of students. In some classrooms students are assumed to be recipients of information. In others they are expected to be creators of knowledge. In the latter case, the students are still recipients of information but they are more fully empowered and engaged. Engaged people tend to learn more than unengaged people. This chapter discusses the emergence of communities in which unity and individuality become mutually reinforcing.

Chapter 7 explores the structures and the processes we use in our approach to teacher professional development. We do this by sharing the stories of the teachers who have joined with us in these attempts to liberate potential and pursue excellence.

An Invitation

Growing up you spent thousands of hours sitting in classrooms, and in most of those classrooms you likely encountered directive approaches to teaching and learning. By the time you entered college, you were already filled with directive assumptions about how to teach. In your education classes and student-teaching experiences, you may have observed more directive practice and learned methods that tend to reinforce the notions of directive practice. After graduation you probably accepted a job at a school whose culture is based on those same directive assumptions. All of this was good. These experiences provided a foundation to get you started in a wonderful profession.

The danger is that you may now be trapped in the assumptions that once facilitated your growth. The beliefs that once served you well may now be holding you back, and you may be losing hope for what you aspired to be. We invite you to consider the stories of the HETs we profile. We invite you to transcend your assumptions and develop a more co-creative perspective of teaching and learning. In this book we share reflection questions, teaching tips from HETs, and other tools to support you in your journey to become the best teacher in you again and again.

CHAPTER 1

Becoming the Best Teacher in You: A Process, Not a Destination

*No punishment anyone lays on you could possibly be worse than
the punishment you lay on yourself by conspiring in your own
diminishment. With that insight comes the ability to open cell doors
that were never locked in the first place.*

— Parker Palmer
The Courage to Teach

IN OUR INTERVIEW WITH KELLI, A VETERAN TEACHER WITH 24 YEARS of experience, she told us about her goal of "reaching every student." While this sentiment is laudable, it also sounded unrealistic, so one of our interviewers decided to push back. He took on the persona of a skeptical colleague and argued that it is unreasonable and unrealistic to expect that a teacher can be successful with every child. Kelli quickly got into the role-play, becoming more passionate as she spoke. She confronted the interviewer: "Why do you have such a negative outlook? It is about you and your expectations for them. You have lowered your expectations. You have given up hope in those kids. What did you think your job was in the first place? It is not about teaching math. It is about getting them to want to learn."

Kelli's intensity and commitment brought about a transformation in the conversation. We were no longer in a role-play. We were having the kind of conversation that causes people to listen deeply, reflect, and see differently—the kind of conversation Kelli creates on a regular basis with her third-grade students.

Becoming the Best Teacher in You

In this chapter Kelli shares her story of becoming a highly effective teacher (HET). Her journey produced an expanded view of herself, her students, and what it means to be a teacher. With this expanded view came the capacity to do things she could not do before. Based on Kelli's story and the stories we have heard from more than 350 other exceptional teachers, we lay out two overarching perspectives of teaching: one we call the directive perspective and the other we call the co-creative perspective. The first is foundational. The second is elusive, but it paves the way for a teacher to accelerate learning and to change lives.

In the exchange above, two things became immediately clear about Kelli. First, she is a person who does not tolerate low expectations. She expects a lot of herself and a lot from others, even interviewers. This also extends to her students. She expects them to do things they do not believe they can do.

Second, while Kelli is a master of her content, she does not believe that her job is only to transfer mathematical information to students. Math is simply a reason to be with her students. She believes that her real job is to create a desire, a hunger, and a love for learning. She expects that her students will leave her with an expanded sense of themselves. They will leave as empowered people, able to learn in any situation.

While Kelli places great emphasis on growth and achievement, she balances it with an equally intense focus on forming and maintaining relationships. Within a few minutes of being with Kelli, we felt like our conversation mattered a great deal and that we also mattered a great deal. We felt both valued and stretched by this woman whom we had just met. She told us that when she was a student, school was a place where you went to "have things done to you." In contrast, Kelli places greater emphasis on doing things *with* her students.

The Year from Hell

Kelli believes that her ability to engage her students is a function of her own development. She speaks of a particularly important episode in which her assumptions about teaching were challenged and ultimately transformed. She came away from the episode with a new view of herself, her students, and what it means to teach.

She told us that her first year of teaching was "stellar." Her second year was "the year from hell." She had many children who were challenging. One was a "belligerent, mouthy, holy terror." On a particularly bad day, she saw him crawling on his belly at the door of her classroom. She lost her temper and moved toward him in anger. As he scurried out of her way, she turned away from him, slammed the door shut, and walked to the principal's office. She told her principal that she could no longer deal with this student, so the student was subsequently removed from her classroom.

This event was deeply troubling to Kelli, so she went to some experienced colleagues for advice. Their advice led to a turning point in Kelli's career. They said, "You have to realize early on that you are not the key to every door."

As Kelli recounted that conversation, she became visibly upset. She fought to compose herself and then looked up and said with conviction, "I hated that." She went on to tell us of a vow she took that day: "I told myself, *I'm not taking that. I'm going to figure out how to meet the needs of those kids.*"

A Vow to Learn

This vow represents a pivotal moment in Kelli's professional life. She could have taken the words of her colleagues to heart and become disenchanted, but she did not. Instead this painful event became an opportunity. It was the beginning of a lifelong journey of learning. In choosing to take this journey, Kelli has developed the ability to work more effectively with difficult students. "I've had other kids like that, but I never had another one of those moments." She described the work she had to do along the way:

I needed to pay more attention to [struggling students]. I had to figure out what works for them, how to have respect for them, how to use humor to diffuse explosive situations. I learned how to make those kinds of kids feel safe in my room, and I learned how to teach them social skills so the other students would feel safe in the room with such a child. And then I learned that I have to be very parent-savvy. I have to sit down and get the parents on my side very early on. So I learned those techniques, and I've never had another year like that. Those seem to be the kids that I'm most drawn to.... I always get those kids now, the most unruly kid, the most disruptive kid, the bully.

Kelli told us that when a difficult child shows up in the school, her administrator says, "Let's put him in Kelli's room because Kelli will know what to do with him."

 TEACHER'S TIP

Kelli: Do not be afraid to engage in new learning. Transformative learning begins to take shape when you engage in your own learning.

- Read qualified authors, observe exemplary teachers, view videos, and meet with other teachers who seem to have mastered what you are struggling with.

- Be willing to forgive yourself for your shortcomings and failures. Vow to make a change and stick with it.

- Seek a partnership with colleagues who will give you encouragement and guidance.

Deep Change

As she pursued her vow, Kelli learned to feel, think, and behave in new ways. She gained new capacity. She went through a learning process that transformed her understanding and aptitude. Robert Quinn, in his work with organizational leaders around the world, has identified two kinds of change that individuals experience: incremental change and deep change.[1]

In our lives and in our work, we frequently make *incremental changes*: We make adjustments, we elaborate on a practice, we try harder, and we exert a greater degree of control. In other words, we attempt to solve the problem using the assumptions we currently hold.

Deep change is more demanding because it requires the surrender of control. It tends to be larger in scope, discontinuous with the past, and irreversible. It involves embracing a purpose and then moving forward by trial and error while attending to real-time feedback. Quinn often refers to the process of deep change as building the bridge as you walk on it.

Kelli knew she wanted to go to another level of performance. She wanted to flourish even with difficult students in the room. To acquire this capacity, she had to first reach for a higher standard and not compromise on that standard as her colleagues advised. Then she had to make a vow to engage in deep change. She moved forward in real-time, experiential learning.

When people move forward in this way, old assumptions are challenged and new ones are constructed. When the new assumptions lead to success, learning often becomes exhilarating. People feel empowered by their success and believe that they can do what Parker Palmer refers to in the epigraph as the ability to "open cell doors that were never locked in the first place."[2]

Slow Death

We often avoid deep change because it can be difficult and unsettling. Ultimately, this avoidance can lead to disengagement, or what Quinn calls "slow death." When Kelli's colleagues told her that she could not expect to be the key to every door, they were unwittingly inviting her to "conspire" in her "own diminishment." They were inviting her to become an active participant in her own slow death.

What these well-meaning colleagues were doing was understandable. They were trying to comfort Kelli in a time of distress. This pattern is a common dynamic among friends and in organizations of all kinds. When people like Kelli aspire to excellence, they often meet adversity and become frustrated. To relieve her distress, Kelli's peers advised her to lower her aspirations. In education, as in all the other industries, this response is a phenomenon that can turn armies of idealistic young professionals into disenchanted victims of the system.

As you think about this dynamic, it is also worthwhile to consider your students' aspirations. Many of them may already travel the path to slow death. Sometimes an entire community of students can be locked into assumptions that prevent them from empowering themselves. What they believe about their ability to learn greatly hinders their own development. Their experiences and the assumptions that result from them can become "cell doors." They may "know," for example, that the act of trying will result in embarrassment and failure. Students who make such assumptions may show little interest in learning. In every industry and in every organization, there are personal and cultural assumptions that lead people away from deep change and toward slow death. Daily conversations that reflect a victim mentality regularly invite us all to the path of slow death.

The Best Teacher in You

Kelli's story illustrates an important point about deep change. Because she engaged in transformative learning, she grew in self-efficacy, or the belief that she could succeed in a demanding situation or activity.[3] More specifically, she is now confident that she can learn to teach any child in any situation. Addressing an imaginary problem child, Kelli told us, "If you are defiant, I will get you. I will figure out what makes you work. I might not get tremendous growth and I might not get engagement every day, but I'm going to get something out of you. I'm going to be your new best friend."

While the statement suggests that Kelli is an empowered person, it also suggests that she is an empowering person. She subjects her students to high expectations, and she also partners with them to help them grow into more-effective versions of themselves. Because she has experienced the realization of her own potential, Kelli sees potential in all of her students and feels compelled to help them change the limiting assumptions that they make about themselves.

When a teacher is with students in a way that is empowering to them, the students can transform. When this begins to happen, the transformation in the students loops back to the teacher and another transformation takes place. The work of teaching becomes the joy of teaching because they are in a mutually empowering relationship. Teachers experience the most powerful of all rewards in this kind of relationship—the realization of their best self, or the best teacher in them. Kelli explains it as follows: "I breathe students. They are my life's blood. I am not whole without them. They bring me joy. They make me frustrated. They make me cry. They give me hope. When I invest in them, I become the best me."

TEACHER'S TIP

Kelli: Ask yourself, *Do I believe that student growth starts with me?* Be strategic about how you make the learning happen in your classroom. As you prepare your lessons and instruction, consider how you can incorporate formative instructional practices.

- Make the learning intentions clear to students. Be sure students understand what you want them to know and be able to do.

- Align assessments with the intended learning and allow students to partner with you on collecting that data.

- Ensure that the feedback you give around the learning is effective. Teach students how to use and give feedback to you and their peers. This strengthens classrooms.

- Allow for opportunities for strong student engagement and ownership of learning. Teach students how to self-assess and set goals. When the vision is clear for students, they can and will join you on the teaching and learning journey.

Transformational Influence

Kelli told us that teaching is about "helping children grow." Kelli said that she can teach a child to read or do math, but that is not what her kind of teaching is about. Her kind of teaching is about helping each child internalize the desire and the ability to learn. With fire in her eyes and conviction in her voice, Kelli stated, "I am the key to every door."

In other fields, such as business or government, the few people with this kind of confidence, passion, and capacity are called *transformational leaders*. They know how to engage people in learning that alters their assumptions and mindsets. They help individuals and groups grow into more-effective versions of themselves. They know how to release potential that is unrecognized and unrealized.

In telling us that she is "the key to every door," Kelli is not claiming that she moves every child forward every minute that they are in her classroom. She is claiming that she is able to enter an elevated state of teaching and learning. She accepts responsibility, faces challenges, and adapts. She does this with confidence, knowing that she can form a relationship with every child; and because of her capacity to do this, she is able to move each child and the class as a whole further than would normally be expected. Kelli has mastered something that can help every teacher become the best teacher they can be. That is why we have written this book.

Two Views of Teaching

Kelli kept surprising us. She kept recounting stories that exceeded our expectations and challenged our assumptions. The same thing happened in our interviews with other HETs, so we began to ask what assumptions are commonly made about the process of teaching.

Because the conventional assumptions of a culture are often reflected in that culture's language, an examination of the dictionary is a good place to start. To teach is to instruct, train, school, discipline, drill, or educate. Consider the meaning of each word.[4]

- ■ *Teach:* to impart knowledge or skill to

- ■ *Instruct:* to provide with knowledge, especially in a methodical way

- *Train:* to coach in or accustom to a mode of behavior or performance

- *School:* to discipline or control

- *Discipline:* to train by instruction and practice, especially to teach self-control to

- *Drill:* to instruct thoroughly by repetition in a skill or procedure

- *Educate:* to develop the innate capacities of, especially by schooling or instruction

These definitions suggest that a teacher directs and controls the classroom. Teaching is a process in which a more expert person imparts knowledge or skill to a less expert person. The student is in a lower position in a knowledge hierarchy. The student is expected to perform to an existing standard or acquire an accustomed mode of behavior or performance. The provision of knowledge is methodical. The student is subjected to discipline and control. The process may be repetitive and should lead to the development of self-control on the part of the student. We call this view the *directive perspective.*

In books it is common to create an image or list and then use it as a straw man. The image is then attacked and replaced by a better image. This book offers a second image, but it does not denigrate the directive perspective. Great teaching is built on a solid foundation of expertise, direction, control, discipline, and repetition. We need the assumptions and the skills of the directive perspective. They are essential to teaching.

The second perspective that we develop later in this chapter is not better than the first. Instead it supplements the directive perspective with additional capacities that make teaching more effective. It values the directive perspective but moves beyond notions such as discipline and repetition. Great music, for example, is a product of more than mechanics, scales, and simple melodies—it is ultimately about finding a unique musical voice and the courage to express it. To do this musicians have to risk, experiment, learn, and create. In their performances great musicians are deeply and dynamically connected to their instrument, their music, and their audience. Similarly, great teachers are deeply and dynamically connected to their subject, their content standards, their evolving practice, and their students. In these dynamic connections, there are feedback loops. Knowledge is not only disseminated but also co-created. The teacher and the student join together to generate knowledge. In this process both the teacher and the student grow.

From Novice to Master

Novelist and philosopher Robert Pirsig asks why, in a given activity, some people obtain normal outcomes while others generate outcomes of higher quality. To answer the question, he uses the metaphor of the motorcycle mechanic. He suggests that not all mechanics are the same; the quality of their work varies:

> Sometime look at a novice workman or a bad workman and compare his expression with that of a craftsman whose work you know is excellent and you'll see the difference. The craftsman isn't ever following a single line of instruction. He's making decisions as he goes along. For that reason he'll be absorbed and attentive to what he is doing even though he does not deliberately contrive this. His motions and the machine are in a kind of harmony. He isn't following any set of written instructions because the nature of the material at hand determines his thoughts and motions, which simultaneously change the nature of the material at hand. The material and his thoughts are changing together in a progression of changes until his mind is at rest at the same time the material is right.[5]

Pirsig is claiming that there are master mechanics (just as there are highly effective teachers) who produce extraordinary outcomes. They do more than act upon an object with expertise. Just as Kelli is "with" her students, the mechanic is "with" the motorcycle in a relationship of reciprocal influence: "The material and his thoughts are changing together in a progression of changes." In this learning relationship, the machine and the mechanic are both altered. The machine is being repaired with excellence while the mechanic is also becoming more excellent. The work of the master mechanic is an intrinsically motivated labor of love because when he does his work, he also produces a better self. He is expressing the best mechanic in him.

Mastery in the Classroom

Excellence is a dynamic process. We take the liberty to rewrite and then elaborate on Pirsig's account with respect to a master teacher to describe what these dynamics look like in the classroom:

> Sometime look at a novice teacher and compare his expression with that of a master teacher whose work you know is excellent, and you'll see the difference. The master teacher isn't ever following a single line of instruction. He has a plan, but it soon becomes a rough guide as he begins to respond to students' needs and to improvise. He is fully present, making decisions as he goes. The master teacher is absorbed and attentive to what he is doing even though he does not deliberately contrive this. His actions and the actions of his students are in a kind of harmony. The master teacher's ongoing assessment of his students determines his thoughts and actions, which simultaneously change the nature of what and how students are learning. The teacher and the class co-create a process of reciprocal, real-time learning. In doing this they are becoming a learning community. This process continues until the teacher's mind is at rest and the particular lesson is concluded with excellence. Both the students and the teacher leave the lesson having had a deeply meaningful learning experience.

As this process unfolds, the teacher recognizes needs, facilitates discussion, builds trust, and inspires spontaneous contributions. The natural hesitancies within students and the natural disparities among students begin to diminish. The conversation becomes more authentic, more engaging, and more reflective. Listening becomes mutual, and students expect one another to contribute.

As in Kelli's story, the classroom becomes a place where students engage in activities that they find relevant and challenging. The teacher improvises and encourages creativity. As the teacher relaxes overt control, the students take ownership of their learning, and leadership shifts seamlessly from one participant to another. Through discussion they explore the big picture and continually question assumptions. Students begin to see from multiple perspectives. In this heightened, collective state, students arrive at creative, joint conclusions. Participating in the process not only builds knowledge but also increases self-efficacy. Students see more potential in themselves and in their world, and they begin to more fully believe in their own capacity to learn and create. They feel more empowered and experience the love of learning. So does the teacher.

As you read our adaptation and the accompanying detail, how did you respond? Did it challenge some of your basic assumptions? If it did, you may have felt skepticism and disbelief. Yet most of us have been part of a group in which this kind of "magic" emerges. We invite you to keep an open mind. As you read *The Best Teacher in You*, if something surprises you, first note exactly what it is. Suspend judgment and then open yourself to possibility. Ask yourself how the surprise might help you enlarge your assumptions and expectations regarding the practice of teaching.

Interconnected Perspectives

Our elaboration of Pirsig's account suggests that teachers—like motorcycle mechanics—need the directive perspective. But if they seek to accelerate learning and change lives, they need to do what Kelli did. They need to be able to transcend their directive assumptions and move into the realm of co-creation. These two perspectives are shown in figure 1.1.

Two Views

Each of these perspectives provides a set of assumptions or lenses for making sense of teaching. Looking through the lens of the directive perspective, learning is a technical process managed by a teacher. It tends to be about content and control. The teacher is in charge—a person in a position of hierarchical authority, who sets high standards while maintaining order. Planning, assessment, and achievement are emphasized. We use the acorn as a metaphor to capture the essence of the directive perspective because it provides the foundation for good teaching. A new teacher often uses the directive perspective to build his or her confidence and capabilities to create an orderly classroom. While the acorn or directive perspective is an important starting point, it comes to life only when it grows into something more dynamic. The directive perspective can be broadened over time to grow into the *co-creative perspective.*

As the teacher and the students commit to a common purpose and form high-quality relationships, they become a system that has emergent

Figure 1.1 *Two Perspectives of Teaching*

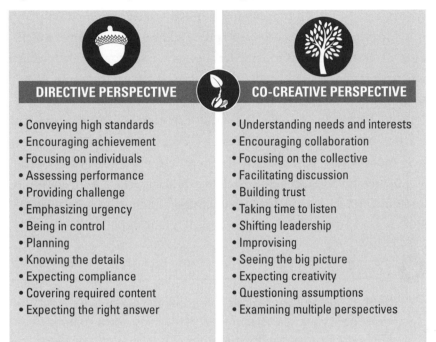

DIRECTIVE PERSPECTIVE	CO-CREATIVE PERSPECTIVE
• Conveying high standards	• Understanding needs and interests
• Encouraging achievement	• Encouraging collaboration
• Focusing on individuals	• Focusing on the collective
• Assessing performance	• Facilitating discussion
• Providing challenge	• Building trust
• Emphasizing urgency	• Taking time to listen
• Being in control	• Shifting leadership
• Planning	• Improvising
• Knowing the details	• Seeing the big picture
• Expecting compliance	• Expecting creativity
• Covering required content	• Questioning assumptions
• Expecting the right answer	• Examining multiple perspectives

possibilities. *Emergent* means something that is embryonic, like a seed, that can then sprout, grow, or develop into something more complex, like a tree. We include the image of the seedling to reinforce that the more dynamic perspective emerges from the acorn. Without the acorn the tree cannot sprout and flourish.

When individual minds become fully engaged and integrated around a common purpose, collaboration can move to a higher level. Learning can grow into something more complex. The group can learn in ways that the individual cannot. When the group is functioning at a high level, the individual may feel that he or she has become part of something bigger than self, something worthy of sacrifice.

When this happens the social structure can transform. In the conventional hierarchy, the belief is that the teacher must hold students accountable. When collaborative learning occurs, students may begin to hold one another accountable. At this moment of transformation, the teacher can move beyond the role of disciplinarian. The network of relationships becomes more flexible, and the classroom, as a functioning whole, can acquire the capacity to co-create and learn more deeply.

To bring about the co-creative process, the teacher becomes a facilitator of learning. In this role the teacher pays attention to relationships and works to create a culture of collaboration, a context that is more likely to give rise to full engagement and accelerated learning.

Kelli gives an example. To establish a culture of "what it is to be a learner" at the beginning of the year, Kelli sets a tone of respect, teaches her students how to be effective listeners, and makes them feel valued. Facilitation involves providing challenge and support, asking questions, and moving back and forth in directive and nondirective ways to enable students to join together in the process of co-creation.

TEACHER'S TIP

Kelli: Challenge yourself as a teacher to change what you view about your role. Is your view of teaching a "true barrier" to moving forward with students? If our view of teaching is limited, we will often become disengaged and unhappy with our job.

Connecting the Two Views

The kind of improvisation a master teacher employs cannot occur without sufficient underlying structure. Teachers still must teach content. They still strive for high achievement. They continue to focus attention on individuals, assess performance, and engage in all the aspects of practice listed on the left side of figure 1.1.

What changes in the co-creative perspective is the teacher's stance relative to students. The teacher is willing to surrender control until it is again necessary to take control. In the directive perspective, the focus is on the teacher and the teaching. In the co-creative perspective, the attention is on the learning of the student rather than the knowledge of the teacher. The co-creative perspective focuses on who the student is becoming and how the teacher can serve as a mediator between where things are and where things could be.

Kelli provides an example of the interconnectedness of the two perspectives. At the beginning of the year, she tries to quickly acclimate students to the rules and the routines of her classroom. Kelli helps students understand the parameters for what and how they will learn. Efficient learning depends on the structures and the fixed processes of the directive perspective. At the same time, Kelli invites students into conversations about "how much you learn, how fast you learn, and the ways in which you learn." She wants to give students a sense of purpose for their own learning. Learning progresses as a journey that Kelli and her students take together.

🖊 *TEACHER'S TIP*

Kelli: Take the time to figure out what students are interested in and use that interest to build a relationship. If it is not something you know about, approach the child as if you are the learner and you want the child to teach you about his or her passion.

Teacher Development

The two perspectives also have implications for how to help teachers improve. From a directive perspective, teacher development is more likely to focus on honing skills related to planning, classroom management, and pedagogy. This perspective assumes that particular practices reliably produce particular outcomes. Professional development in this perspective relies on experts to provide teachers with scientifically validated solutions to predictable pedagogic problems. All of this is true, but it is also partial by itself.

In the co-creative perspective, a classroom becomes an adaptive organization. It consists of people in relationships with one another. Each student is an interdependent actor with the potential to learn, teach, and know. Learning accelerates and is deepened when a teacher forms high-quality relationships with students. Learning accelerates further when students form high-quality relationships with one another. To achieve this level of relationship, the teacher continually clarifies purpose, increases authenticity, practices empathy, and opens to the co-creative journey.

Teacher development, in the co-creative perspective, is likely to focus on reflection, self-assessment, interaction, experimentation, and learning from experience.[6] Teachers engage in activities that challenge them and invite them to examine their own assumptions and beliefs. They are encouraged to empower themselves to explore, appreciate, and integrate alternative assumptions. These experiences enable them to think and act in more complex ways. As they build these capacities, they better understand how to empower students and accelerate learning. Here a teaching practice is not so much a solution to a problem as an opportunity for experimentation, engagement, and learning.

In the co-creative perspective, development is not teaching teachers to know; it is teaching teachers to learn. As a teacher develops the capacity to think and act in more complex ways, his or her effectiveness increases because effectiveness is a function of being in the present and learning to adapt and create in real time. The objective is for the teacher to acquire adaptive confidence and transformational influence.

Reality

Researchers suggest that 10,000 is the magic number of hours needed to attain mastery.[7] If a gifted pianist, for example, puts in 9,000 hours of practice, that person is likely to have a less luminary career than a gifted musician who puts in 10,000 hours. Ten thousand hours seems to be a threshold.

By the time we graduate from college, we all have more than 10,000 hours in classrooms observing teachers. This extensive socialization means we are all deeply rooted in the directive view of teaching. As we have seen, the directive perspective is at the heart of our experiences, language, and culture. To access the co-creative perspective, we have to undergo deep change and experience transformative learning. In this book you will find stories, concepts, and tools to help you do just that.

Summary

Highly effective teachers like Kelli have daunting challenges. They work with the same students in the same schools with the same resources as other teachers. Their organizational context is hierarchical, conflict-ridden, and politically charged. And while these challenges lead some teachers to feel frustrated, discouraged, and dissatisfied, highly effective teachers somehow learn to perform at high levels.

Through our work with HETs, we have tried to make sense of what accounts for their extraordinary impact. To do this we have drawn from a number of different scientific literatures to develop some hypotheses about the integration of the directive and co-creative perspectives. This book shares our theories with you. Chapter 2 introduces a framework that will help you more deeply examine and reflect on HETs' journeys from novice to master teacher so that you can begin to apply these lessons to your own teaching practice.

🌰 *PLANTING SEEDS*

1. Kelli says, "It is not about teaching math. It is about getting them to want to learn." What are the implications of working toward the one purpose versus the other? How might the two purposes be integrated?

2. Kelli started out well, but her students changed and her assumptions did not. This led to failure and frustration. Her friends advised her, "You have to realize early on that you are not the key to every door." When have you received or given such advice? What arguments justify this advice? How is accepting such advice conspiring in your own diminishment?

3. Kelli made a vow that took her on a new path. She states:

   > I needed to pay more attention to those types of kids. I had to figure out what works for them, how to have respect for them, how to use humor to diffuse explosive situations. I learned how to make those kinds of kids feel safe in my room, and I learned how to teach them social skills so the other students would feel safe in the room with such a child. And then I

learned that I have to be very parent-savvy. I have to sit down and get the parents on my side very early on. So I learned those techniques, and I've never had another year like that.

How is this kind of learning different from the procedural learning to which we are more accustomed? What are the key requirements for this kind of learning? What does this suggest about your most pressing frustrations?

GROWING YOUR PRACTICE

1. What is one specific practice you can undertake in your next week of teaching to build momentum on the journey to the co-creative perspective? Use the right-hand column in figure 1.1 to help you identify a specific practice. Be specific about when, who, what, and how you will get started.

2. Following Kelli's advice, identify one student whom you would like to reach in a deeper way. Find out what he or she is interested in and use that interest to build a relationship. If it is not something you know about, approach the child as if you are the learner and you want the child to teach you about his or her passion.

CHAPTER 2

Embracing Connections: Integrating Essential Elements

Paradoxical thinking requires that we embrace a view of the world in which opposites are joined, so that we can see the world clearly and see it whole. Such a view is characterized by neither flinty-eyed realism nor dewy-eyed romanticism but rather by a creative synthesis of the two.... The result is a world more complex and confusing than the one made simple by either-or thought—but simplicity is merely the dullness of death. When we think things together, we reclaim the life force in the world, in our students, in ourselves.

—Parker Palmer
The Courage to Teach

DIANA IS AN EIGHTH-GRADE SCIENCE TEACHER IN A RURAL SCHOOL district. She has been teaching for more than 25 years. From the moment our interview started, we knew that we were encountering someone who "thinks things together." In our interview Diana used the word *connection* over and over. She believes that making new connections between ideas has many important payoffs. She told us it provides a sense of control over your life, a sense of peace within yourself, and a sense of life satisfaction.

Diana not only connects ideas; she also connects with people and makes connections between people. As Diana spoke of her love for her subject and her students, we found ourselves drawn to her as we were drawn to Kelli. At the outset of our interview, Diana said something that seemed linked to the enthusiasm we were experiencing. She told us she was not interested "in a life of survival." She is not happy to "just exist." She said, "I want to flourish."

Diana told us she also wants her students to flourish. Like Kelli, helping her students become lifelong learners is a central part of Diana's life purpose. She believes that this purpose can be fulfilled only if she is constantly learning, and she believes that learning is accelerated and deepened by making connections at every level.

CHAPTER OVERVIEW

Embracing Connections

In this chapter Diana's story provides an illustration of teaching that creates connections at multiple levels. To explain these connections, we introduce the BFK•Connect Framework (referred to as the *Connect Framework* in this book), which identifies four core dimensions of effective teaching. With these dimensions defined, the framework also provides the ingredients for what might be called "integrative" or "powerful" practice. The Connect Framework is a tool that can help you engage in paradoxical thinking and see new possibilities. As you do, you may find that you are better able to make connections that accelerate learning in your students and in yourself.

Connecting the Two Perspectives

Diana spends considerable time thinking about how to link new ideas with the ideas that are already in her students' minds. Sometimes she is explicit about the process and assists students in seeing the connections. She informs (akin to the directive perspective). At other times she sends students off on their own to discover the key connections. She empowers students to create their own understanding (akin to the co-creative perspective). As she reflected on her success in terms of high value-added scores, she said, "I think that's why they do better. I evolve them."

Diana works to turn her students into more empowered and effective versions of themselves, people who can make creative connections and learn on their own. As she teaches them, she says each insight provides a bit of energy, and they light up. In commenting on the feel-good effects of "lighting up," she makes another observation about connections and a self-reinforcing process that helps her turn students into lifelong learners:

> You see that light bulb come on in kids. You see them understand or make a connection visually in their eyes, or verbally they'll say, "Oh." That gives you chills as a teacher to know that you really hit a nerve with them. And when you hit those nerves, you wake those nerves up and they want that again. It is stimulating their brains, and they enjoy that. It is a good feeling. I know what it feels like. I want them to feel it. I think the more nerves I touch and the more times they feel it, the more they want it and the more they're going to become lifelong learners [who are] self-motivated.

When students first join her classroom, most of them do not share Diana's passion for science. She does not see this as a flaw in her students; she sees it as an opportunity to develop that desire. This process does not begin with her acting on the students. It begins with her acting upon herself. She does the internal work necessary to display her own enjoyment of learning. She claims that by demonstrating her own love of learning, she forms an emotional connection with students and "opens them up to what it feels like" to make new connections. Her excitement for learning becomes contagious. Diana does not just want students to learn new information (directive perspective); she also wants them to feel the excitement of making their own connections and discoveries (co-creative perspective).

Diana also speaks of making another kind of interpersonal connection that increases her likelihood of being successful with students. She practices empathy. She disciplines herself to imagine how her students might feel when she engages in a particular behavior. This practice psychologically connects her to her students. She joins with them in a new system of learning, wherein she and her students are connected in a loop that allows her to learn as she teaches: "I really try to empathize; I really try to be at one with them and on their level and connect with them.... I care about them....I try to put myself in their place. What would *I* want to see? How would *I* learn? How would *I* get it? You have to constantly pique my interest or I'm going to be bored, so I try to constantly do the same with them, and that's where I'm learning."

As part of this interdependent, co-creative process, Diana helps her students articulate their interests. As a facilitator she finds ways to help students ask the questions they "really care about." This phrase is important. It suggests that in her classroom, directive discussions about science become more authentic conversations. Authentic questions reflect genuine interests, and the conversations become more relevant. Engagement increases, and more dynamic teaching and learning patterns tend to emerge.

◐ *TEACHER'S TIP*

Diana: Think about your lesson on the way to and from work.

- Rehearse the general flow of what you plan to do.
- Work on "weak spots" that you anticipate being less engaging.
- Put yourself in your students' shoes. Would you enjoy the lesson? Is it clear and easy to understand yet still interesting?

The students, for example, raise questions that surprise Diana. The questions sometimes exceed her ability to answer. While some teachers might dread these moments and fear they will undermine their authority, Diana seeks to stimulate these kinds of questions. She sees them as a sign that she is succeeding. They indicate that the conversation is leaving the realm of the known and moving to a more meaningful place on the boundary between order and chaos. In these kinds of conversations, the students and the teacher both become more vulnerable. They are interdependent equals in the search for knowledge. In such a process, vulnerability is a strength that accelerates learning: "That's where I do a lot of my learning....It's like, 'Oh, I never thought about that' or 'You know, that's a good question. That is a really good question.' So that's the natural evolution of the learning process in the classroom; it's their responses, their questions, the situations that come up that you don't expect. That's where most of the learning takes place....As I'm planning my teaching, as I'm executing it, all these new questions come up and there is just constant learning."

Diana uses another important phrase. She speaks of the *natural evolution of the learning process.* Diana's language describes how new patterns emerge, which is at the heart of the co-creative perspective. In this process her role as authority figure fades into the background, and the normal hierarchy goes dormant. Here, again, she emphasizes her equality with students: "Teachers don't know it all. It's not a bad thing. We can learn together, right along with them, and sometimes it's not the answer that's important; it's what you learn in the search."

In the search there is another transformational dynamic: Diana is no longer the center of attention, and neither are the students. At the center of attention is the process of learning. The class transforms from a hierarchy to an adaptive learning organization.

TEACHER'S TIP

Diana: It is very easy to get caught up in teaching the content that we are expected to teach and to focus on test results used to "evaluate" our effectiveness as teachers. What we fail to realize is that if we relax and make frequent connections to life experiences, the content and the positive results naturally follow. If students cannot relate to the material being taught, most of it will be forgotten despite our best efforts. Connections help students not only learn material but use it to make their lives better.

- **Ask your students to make connections to their own lives.** Praise them when they make these connections on their own. Help them when they are having trouble making connections on their own.

- **Give them examples of how the learning relates to their lives or ways that you have applied the ideas in your life.** I enjoy sharing stories about my travels around the world, our farm animals and all the gory details, my family, hunting experiences, and anything that can help my students make connections.

It is painful at times and takes much longer than the traditional "sit and get" style, but it cements their learning and gives meaning to what you are trying to share. While doing this our lives become richer, deeper, and more meaningful in the process. Students share their connections, and we begin to make logical sense of what we are teaching and why it truly is important. It is then that teaching becomes our lives, not our jobs, and we teach people, not content.

In the shift from hierarchy to an adaptive learning system, conversations *emerge* and activities *self-organize*. Diana finds herself needing to say less. The students own the classroom experience, and she is able to sit back and listen to them as they engage the learning process. At times she may redirect with some of the basic concepts from class (directive perspective), but the students are creating discussions with one another (co-creative perspective). Diana declares, "That type of setting is usually what I feel is the best learning because they're learning from each other."

TEACHER'S TIP

Diana: You have to plan lessons and put a lot of thought into how to best allow students to discover as much as possible on their own. It is not easy to do, but with practice everyone can master the skill of helping students uncover ideas on their own. This hard work pays off when students light up as they make these discoveries. It builds self-esteem and teaches skills that set up students to become lifelong learners. You have to give them foundations and skills, but then you have to let them apply them on their own. We sometimes take our work too personally and are unwilling to veer from our intended lesson. If a lesson is not going the way you think it should, change it midstream. If it takes an unexpected turn, follow it. The unexpected learning is sometimes the richest.

Throughout the interview Diana demonstrated a capacity for para-doxical thinking. *Paradoxical thinking* is the ability to integrate things that are normally separated. Diana exemplifies this perspective. For example, she integrates the notion of teacher and student as two elements of the same larger, dynamic learning system.

A Framework

In life we are always dividing things into discrete categories and then putting them back together again. In the language of human develop-ment, this is called *differentiating and integrating*. For example, when teachers introduce a complex concept in class, they frequently break down the learning into smaller components (differentiating) and then scaffold the learning to build the pieces back into a whole (integrating). As people become more masterful in any given domain of activity, they increase their ability to differentiate the whole into even more pieces and then to reintegrate those pieces back into a conceptual whole. Diana, like Pirsig's master motorcycle mechanic, has an ability to be with her students in complex ways that give rise to outcomes of excellence. Here we introduce a framework that may help you in thinking about what it means to differentiate and integrate.

In the early HET workshops, Mike Thomas and other Battelle for Kids (BFK) colleagues found themselves engaged in a process of differentiating and integrating. As they probed teachers and listened to their discussions about teaching and learning, they recorded long lists of practices, intentions, and stories. For two years they pored over the lists until four themes emerged. They found they could split almost all of what they heard into four general categories.[1]

- **Relationships:** cultivating a supportive community

- **Continuous improvement:** adapting and embracing change

- **High expectations:** maximizing every student's achievement

- **Stable environment:** creating structures and processes

These categories implicitly suggest four underlying human needs: belonging, growth, accomplishment, and security. The four general categories allow us to use "either/or thinking" to logically distinguish many practices. As an illustration, recall the list of practices associated with the directive and co-creative perspectives. Each of the practices in the two perspectives can be placed in one of the above four categories as shown in figure 2.1.

The ability to categorize what they heard was useful, but Mike and his colleagues were puzzled by something else they observed. The workshop participants—people like Kelli and Diana—rarely talked about these categories in isolation. While they might begin by sharing an effective teaching practice that could be placed in one category, their description of the practice would often bleed over into the other categories. When some

Figure 2.1 *Practices Associated with the Directive and Co-Creative Perspectives*

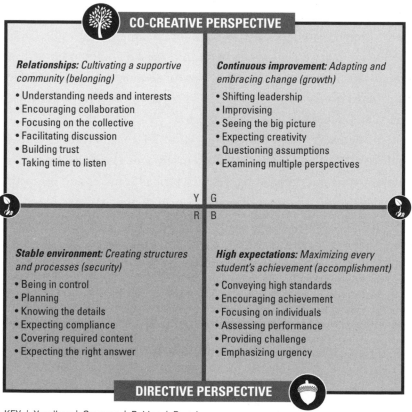

CO-CREATIVE PERSPECTIVE

Relationships: *Cultivating a supportive community (belonging)*
- Understanding needs and interests
- Encouraging collaboration
- Focusing on the collective
- Facilitating discussion
- Building trust
- Taking time to listen

Continuous improvement: *Adapting and embracing change (growth)*
- Shifting leadership
- Improvising
- Seeing the big picture
- Expecting creativity
- Questioning assumptions
- Examining multiple perspectives

Y | G
R | B

Stable environment: *Creating structures and processes (security)*
- Being in control
- Planning
- Knowing the details
- Expecting compliance
- Covering required content
- Expecting the right answer

High expectations: *Maximizing every student's achievement (accomplishment)*
- Conveying high standards
- Encouraging achievement
- Focusing on individuals
- Assessing performance
- Providing challenge
- Emphasizing urgency

DIRECTIVE PERSPECTIVE

KEY | Y: yellow | G: green | B: blue | R: red

teachers described their practices, the boundaries between the categories seemed to soften and the practices began to connect in self-reinforcing ways.[2] This realization led Mike and his colleagues to think about teaching in terms of a well-established framework that both differentiates and integrates effective organizational and leadership practice: the Competing Values Framework (CVF).

The CVF came from empirical research done by Robert Quinn and John Rohrbaugh in 1983 and has since been applied to many subjects and contexts.[3] From the data collected at our HET workshops, we developed a competing values framework of educational practices. We eventually honed a simplified version called the BFK•Connect Framework, which can be seen on the inside front cover of this book.

The relationships quadrant (yellow) emphasizes things like collaboration, support, respect, and care. The continuous improvement quadrant (green) emphasizes such things as adaptability, visioning, relevance, creativity, and experimentation. The high expectations quadrant (blue) emphasizes things like goal setting, accountability, assessment, and achievement. The stable environment quadrant (red) emphasizes structures, routines, efficiency, and management. The four quadrants are summarized in figure 2.2.

In working with teachers, we found that the colors used in the framework (see the inside front cover) are useful. The colors help teachers remember the four categories, and teachers frequently refer to the quadrants by color. The remainder of the book presents various versions of the framework in black-and-white but continues to refer to the quadrants by the colors shown on the inside cover. You can also download a color copy of the framework from BestTeacherinYou.org.

Making the connection to the CVF was an important step because it provided a way to connect and integrate the four lists of distinct practices in ways that correspond with how HETs connected these practices. The connections are shown as the vertical and horizontal lines that divide the framework into the four quadrants (figure 2.2). The vertical line represents the need to balance flexibility and openness with order and control. This tension comes into play as teachers decide how much

Figure 2.2 *Descriptions of the BFK•Connect Framework Quadrants*

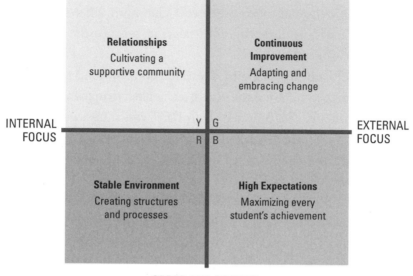

KEY | Y: yellow | G: green | B: blue | R: red

structure to incorporate as they organize their classrooms and develop learning activities. The horizontal line represents the need to balance the relationship between internal and external issues. This tension comes into play as teachers decide where to focus their attention. An internal focus directs attention to dynamics within the classroom such as the classroom environment and students' individual needs, whereas an external focus draws attention to demands coming from outside the classroom such as state standards and assessments.

Because the four categories are distinct, they are often viewed as competing with one another. Yet the framework recognizes that all four categories are necessary. Effectiveness, in terms of this framework, requires teachers to integrate the four distinct categories. That is why we emphasize connection in the title of the framework. The tool is meant to help teachers make connections across four core categories of effectiveness. The quadrants are not dissociated dimensions of teaching and learning; they are different facets of effective practice that can be connected in practical and powerful ways in the classroom.

Four Dimensions of Effective Practice

As we worked with the Connect Framework, we began to think of the classroom as an organization and the teacher as a leader. To ensure that this logic made sense to teachers, we shared the framework with groups of HETs in our workshops in subsequent years. The framework resonated with them as a useful lens for making sense of their practice. The vertical and horizontal tensions represented in the framework and the resulting four dimensions of effectiveness are all important issues to classroom teachers. At the same time, the framework gives educators a common language to describe different aspects of their practice. Building from the framework, we were able to articulate a set of operating assumptions, or a theory of practice, associated with each quadrant.

Yellow Quadrant: Relationships

The upper-left quadrant emphasizes relationships and the creation of a cohesive learning organization. Practices in the yellow quadrant are grounded in the idea that students need to feel a sense of belonging. The implicit goal is collaborative capacity. Learning is characterized as a collective process that is accelerated by building trust. The objective is for students to become a team characterized by mutual respect with an emphasis on learning together. The culture is marked by positive relationships. The teacher tends to be empathic and able to work with the individual concerns of each student. The time orientation is more long-term, and the teacher invests time in building relationships. The classroom organization is a clan or network of trusting relationships. A key process is the facilitation of collective dialogue. Instead of telling, the teacher asks meaningful questions and listens.[4] In such a classroom, transactional assumptions of justice are replaced by the practice of positive regard. One teacher, for example, told us, "When a student is disrespectful, I correct them while modeling complete respect for the student."

As is the case with each of these quadrants, a strongly enacted perspective can become a liability. The risk in the extreme application of a yellow quadrant theory of action is that excessive concern can turn into coddling, collusion, and work avoidance. When this happens the classroom becomes less effective. The blue quadrant in particular can help teachers avoid moving into this negative zone.

Green Quadrant: Continuous Improvement

The upper-right quadrant emphasizes novelty and the creation of a generative learning organization. *Generative* in this sense means creative and naturally evolving. Practices in the green quadrant are grounded in the idea that students need to grow. The implicit goal is the ability to self-actualize, to become a self-empowered, lifelong learner. Learning is characterized as a spontaneous process that is accelerated through the co-creation of new processes. The objective is to establish an adaptive and flexible classroom that is a stimulating environment for learning. In this generative domain, the emphasis is on creative exploration and relevance, and the culture is marked by high engagement. The teacher tends to be a catalyst of transformation. The time orientation is forward-looking, and students are encouraged to envision and realize potential in real time. They bring the future into the present. The emphasis is less on facts and more on examining and questioning assumptions and beliefs so that learning is transformative. The organization is less hierarchical and more of an agile structure that flexes as necessary. The desire is for students to develop a love for learning. Key processes are self-organization and shared leadership. In such a classroom, leadership moves from person to person as the teacher sometimes disappears from the center of attention and control. One teacher told us, "They discover the lesson among themselves and leave me with little to do but watch in amazement."

A green theory of action also has limitations. An excessive application of green quadrant attributes can result in a loss of control or the emergence of chaos and disorder. As is the case with any of these quadrants, when green attributes are overemphasized the classroom becomes less effective. The red quadrant in particular can help teachers avoid moving into this negative zone.

Blue Quadrant: High Expectations

The lower-right quadrant emphasizes achievement and the creation of a performance-focused learning organization. Practices in the blue quadrant are grounded in the idea that students need to feel a sense of accomplishment. The implicit goal is to have students develop self-efficacy and persistence. Learning is characterized as an individualized process that is accelerated through goal setting and accountability. The objective is to challenge and stretch each student. The culture is marked by measurable progress. The teacher tends to be task-focused, and the time orientation suggests urgency. Every moment is used productively. There may be a sense of competition. What matters most is the ability to produce results. The desire is for high test scores, and the means to that end is personal discipline. The teacher is a motivator of effort. Two of the key blue quadrant processes are goal setting and assessment, and the expected outcome is progress. In such a classroom, students and teacher put forth tremendous effort. One teacher told us, "My students know that I notice when they've worked hard…but I also notice when they haven't worked hard, when they haven't worked to their potential."

When blue quadrant attributes are overemphasized, expectations can become so high and demands so intense that students become discouraged, alienated, and frustrated. When this happens, a less effective classroom is the result. The yellow quadrant in particular can help teachers avoid moving into this negative zone.

Red Quadrant: Stable Environment

The lower-left quadrant emphasizes predictability and the creation of a stable learning organization. Practices in the red quadrant are grounded in the idea that students need security and consistency. The implicit goal is to have students develop self-control. Learning is characterized as a process that is controlled and that can be accelerated with the right structures, rules, and routines. The objective is to organize the classroom so that it is an efficient environment for learning. There are clear expectations for students, and the culture is marked by high reliability. Students have a sense of order. The time orientation is anchored in the past, as students draw on knowledge that has already been created. The emphasis tends to be on facts and accuracy. The organization is a hierarchy, with the teacher as a manager and the students as subordinates. The desire is for consistent conduct, which is derived from internalizing routines. The marker of success is structure and continuous good conduct. One teacher told us that her routines were so internalized that "If I am not there, the class starts without me." In such a classroom, chaos has been managed into order.

Red quadrant attributes can also be overemphasized. In the extreme application of these attributes, there is a risk of boredom and stagnation. This kind of over-organizing and over-regimenting leads to a less effective classroom. The green quadrant in particular can help teachers avoid moving into this negative zone.

Powerful Practice

For some teachers, like Kelli and Diana, each of these four dimensions is essential, continuously active, and related to all the others. While directive, either/or thinking leads us to differentiate the four dimensions, the dynamic and complex logic of the co-creative perspective suggests that these are complementary dimensions that can be integrated. As teachers like Kelli and Diana develop, they learn to connect the quadrants and engage in what we call *powerful practice.*[5]

Teachers may start out their careers predisposed to one quadrant of the Connect Framework. Depending on their experiences, they may become more open to and more capable in other quadrants. As this happens the teacher begins to engage in more paradoxical thinking and more complex behaviors. This ability to make connections across the framework seems to matter. Organizational research, for example, shows that executives with the ability to work across the framework are more-effective leaders.[6]

In our workshops many teachers identified one quadrant in the model as their "home." Some HETs describe their home quadrant as the dimension that best aligns with their personalities. They realize that *If I try to teach like somebody else, it won't work.* This belief suggests that the journey to mastery is a journey during which we seek to discover and express our best and most unique self. In the remaining chapters, we use the framework to more clearly outline the processes and supports that have helped other HETs develop into their best selves. The best teacher in you is an elevated version of your current self. It may be a version that is more complex, more dynamic, and more unique. Perhaps it is a self that is continuously emerging and has to be continually reconstructed. This may explain why it is so hard for researchers to find linear relationships between teaching practices and effectiveness.[7] Directive logic and research methods may not be appropriate for capturing the complex, dynamic, and unique nature of effective teaching.[8]

✿ TEACHER'S TIP

Diana: Use the styles, techniques, and practices from the quadrant that you are comfortable with, but be sure to reflect on those that you are not as comfortable with or as likely to use. Seek out colleagues who are good at these quadrants and ask what techniques they would use. Pick a few out and try them!

Another way that teachers talk about their home quadrant is as the starting point for their practice or the "frame for everything else to come together," and over time they learn how to "fit the rest in." When teachers begin to integrate the attributes in their home quadrant with the attributes in the other quadrants, it appears that their capacity to be effective expands. Given that these teachers have different starting points, it is reasonable to assume that multiple paths exist to uncover the best teacher within.

Diana provides an illustration of this process. She attributes her success with students to her ability to simultaneously address all four quadrants in her teaching practice. We have inserted references to the quadrants in her statement: "I think that's how my valued-added [blue quadrant] has done well because I give kids what they need [yellow quadrant]. I try to be creative, and I try to be flexible [green quadrant]. I let them know I care [yellow quadrant], yet I have some order to me [red quadrant], and I have high expectations [blue quadrant]....That's how I'm effective because I balance that all subconsciously in my mind without thinking about it."

What is striking about the above statement is that Diana operates across all four of the quadrants "without thinking about it." Integration is natural to her. She moves across the quadrants, creating synergies as she goes.

Synergy

The word *synergy* comes from Greek, and it means "a working with."[9] It suggests a relationship in which two systems begin to connect and interpenetrate in such a way that each enhances the other. The whole becomes greater than the sum of its parts. Pirsig's masterful motorcycle mechanic is "working with" the engine, and the masterful teacher is "working with" students and the processes of learning.

RESEARCH FOUNDATIONS

Synergy

The concept of synergy was first introduced to the social sciences by anthropologist Ruth Benedict.[10] She analyzed communities of Native Americans and noted that while some cultures seemed vital, others seemed to deplete the energy of their members. She wrote, "The conclusion emerges that societies where non-aggression is conspicuous have social orders in which the individual by the same act and at the same time serves his own advantage and that of the group… not because people are unselfish and put social obligations above personal desires, but when social arrangements make these identical."

She is suggesting that in some communities the social obligations and personal desires are connected in a mutually reinforcing loop. In such situations, duty becomes delight and work becomes pleasure. These communities have a shared vitality and energy.

Abraham Maslow was greatly influenced by Ruth Benedict.[11] At one point he studied people who experienced self-actualization. They were people of high character who were creative and potent. He observed that his research participants often transcended normal dichotomies. Work and pleasure, for example, could not be differentiated in these research participants because they were doing what they loved—for them, work was pleasure.

Maslow made the seemingly paradoxical claims that his self-actualizing subjects were often both concrete and abstract, serious and humorous, introverted and extroverted, intense and casual, mystic and realistic, active and passive, masculine and feminine, and so on. Because people are more predisposed to differentiate than to integrate, Maslow's claim may seem perplexing. This kind of paradox was also evident in how Kelli described her relationship with her students in chapter 1. Her students bring her joy and frustration; they make her cry and give her hope. Without them, Kelli does not feel "whole." When she invests in them, she says, "I become the best me." Perhaps what Maslow was trying to say is that self-actualizing people become more complex, adaptive systems. In other words, perhaps self-actualizing people are able to live and work out of all four quadrants.

Consider Diana, the woman who is not interested in survival but instead wants to flourish. For her, teaching is pleasure. She loves what she does. She challenges her students and expects them to make connections on their own. The students are also supported. They feel her love. She provides them with structure, but she is continually improvising with them. The self-actualizing Diana has a powerful "life force" because she is an evolving person who is continuously learning. Diana's ability to create synergies sometimes gives rise to something she calls the "living beast."

TEACHER'S TIP

Diana: Ask yourself these questions:

- Is teaching something you do for your students *and* for yourself?
- Are you teaching content or students?
- Are you preparing students for a test or for life?

The Living Beast

The living beast is a heightened state of collective learning. When the beast emerges, Diana and her students are immersed in the "magic" of learning. While Diana plays a role in bringing about this process, she says she cannot control it. She says it is bigger than she is. In fact, she becomes part of the beast, as do her students. The beast has a life of its own:

> There is just this magical chemistry that happens, and you can't predict when it's going to be. The frequency, I would say, is at least four days out of five, at least one of my classes will run very smoothly and you'll really feel that magic. But it's not every class, every day; it's not every class on a particular day. It's a living, breathing thing that evolves, so you can't predict it with accuracy. Even if you set up the environment to create that magic, it doesn't always happen. And sometimes when you think it's going to be the worst day and you just wish you wouldn't even have stepped out of bed, things go wonderfully well, and that's the type of thing that really keeps you wanting to teach.

While this description may seem strange, in this book you will read other, similar descriptions. Many of the teachers we interviewed spoke of this process but struggled to describe it. Powerful practice seems to be associated with this elusive process of emergent, collective learning.

Mihaly Csikszentmihalyi is a psychologist who studied individual learning at its peak. He identified something he called the *flow state*.[12] Individuals enter the flow state when they have a clear goal. In pursuing the goal, the person gets immediate feedback, knows how he or she is doing, and understands how to adjust to stay on target. Flow tends to occur when the person feels challenged but skilled. Csikszentmihalyi writes:

> When goals are clear, feedback relevant, and challenges and skills are in balance, attention becomes ordered and fully invested. Because of the total demand on psychic energy, a person in flow is completely focused. There is no space in consciousness for distracting thoughts, irrelevant feelings. Self-consciousness disappears, yet one feels stronger than usual. The sense of time is distorted: hours seem to

pass by in minutes. When a person's entire being is stretched in the full functioning of body and mind, whatever one does becomes worth doing for its own sake; living becomes its own justification. In the harmonious focusing of physical and psychic energy, life finally comes into its own.[13]

In this elevated state of learning, people flourish. Flow can occur during a variety of activities, including writing, playing a sport, or doing surgery.

When Diana talks about the dance that gives rise to the "living beast" in her classroom, the focus is not on individual learning. It is on collective learning. The living beast is a process of group flow.[14] To facilitate the emergence of this dynamic state, Diana takes the pulse of her students: "You have to constantly read the kids; you have to read their receptiveness; you have to read their interest; you have to read their current condition as they come into your room.... You read that through their body language, their facial expressions, their conversation with you, their eye contact. So I read that constantly. I'm checking their pulse all the time."

The capacity to read each student as the group is focused on even higher levels of learning is another example of working across quadrants. When there is some degree of structure from the red quadrant, and the trust of the yellow quadrant is deeply intertwined with the focus and the tenacity of the blue quadrant, the magic of the green quadrant may emerge. Collective flow gives rise to creative collaboration. Learning is co-created. Living in such a community may be a key to the acceleration of learning reflected in high value-added scores.

Summary

Diana sees the categories, differences, and oppositions that we all see. But, in keeping with the epigraph from Parker Palmer, Diana tends to "embrace a view of the world in which opposites are joined." This capacity comes from the fact that Diana has a passionate purpose. It propels her into a state of constant learning and enables her to see and create wholes from the connection of parts. Because she "thinks things together," Diana radiates a more intense life force. She turns her classroom into a complex and co-creative organization. It is both safe and challenging. It is conducive to enriched conversations and to the emergence of the living beast. She engages in powerful practice, and her students learn at an accelerated rate.

🌰 PLANTING SEEDS

1. Diana told us she was not interested "in a life of survival." She is not happy to "just exist." She said, "I want to flourish." She also wants her students to flourish. She recognizes that this purpose can be fulfilled only if she is constantly learning and making new connections. Identify one person in your life who is surviving and one person who is flourishing. How do they differ? Where are you on the continuum between survival and flourishing? Where would you like to be, and how might you get there?

2. Diana says she spends considerable time thinking about how to link new ideas with the ideas that are already in her students' minds. Sometimes she assists them, and sometimes she lets her students discover the connections on their own. She says, "I think that's why they do better. I evolve them." What does it mean to evolve? What do connections have to do with evolution?

3. As a facilitator Diana finds ways to help her students ask the questions they "really care about." The resulting questions thus reflect authentic interests and give rise to genuine conversations. What does it mean to be a facilitator? How are genuine conversations different? What do they contribute to learning?

4. In Diana's conversations with her students, they raise questions that surprise her and often exceed her ability to answer. Instead of discouraging the pattern, she seeks to stimulate it. She wants them to ask questions she cannot answer because she becomes vulnerable. What is vulnerability, and why does Diana think it accelerates learning? Why do most people fear being vulnerable?

5. Diana often refers to collective learning as the "living beast." When the beast emerges, Diana and her students are immersed in the "magic" of learning. While Diana plays a role in bringing about

the emergence of the living beast, she cannot control it. She is just a contributor who tries to set the conditions of emergence. What does the word *magic* mean here? When have you experienced magic in your classroom?

 ## GROWING YOUR PRACTICE

1. Reread the descriptions of the four quadrants of the Connect Framework in the section of this chapter titled Four Dimensions of Effective Practice. With which quadrant do you most strongly identify? You may also want to complete the Reflect Assessment (Resource A at the back of the book). The Reflect Assessment helps you identify your strengths and growth opportunities relative to the four quadrants of the framework.

2. Consider doing a thought experiment to take the pulse of the teaching and learning taking place in your school. Imagine walking through the school and observing the body language in each classroom. How many classes would be vital and full of energy? How many classes would appear depleted? Assess your own classroom. What one practice could you develop to bring energy to *your* classroom?

CHAPTER 3

Opening the Mind:
Embracing Deep Change

*Your assumptions are your windows on the world. Scrub them off
every once in a while, or the light won't come in.*

— Alan Alda
Commencement speech at
Connecticut College, 1980

ARON HAS BEEN A TEACHER FOR 15 YEARS AND NOW TEACHES JUNIOR
high math. What he loves most about his profession is interacting
with kids. He seeks to draw out their enthusiasm and give them a vision of
entering into a math occupation when they grow up. He uses that vision
to draw his students into the world of mathematics:

> As we enter a much more competitive global marketplace, there are a
> lot of students overseas who are willing to do a lot more work for a lot
> less money. What is going to separate my students from those other
> students? What is going to get my students careers and the ability to
> support their family and to contribute to society? It all rests on what
> happens in my 42 minutes....So [I] come in, do the best [I] can, and
> [I] hope it's enough, and if it's not, [I] look for ways to get better.

This is a statement of purpose, accountability, and a willingness to
learn. The willingness to learn is important. Aaron is now a highly effective teacher. Yet this was not always the case. He had to learn his way to
increased capacity. He tells stories of struggle and failure, particularly
with the red quadrant. He had to "scrub" some of his assumptions about
how to teach before the "light" was able to "come in."

CHAPTER OVERVIEW

Opening the Mind

In this chapter we use Aaron's story to describe a typical journey for many beginning teachers. To become more effective, they often must first discover how to organize and manage the learning in their classrooms. Many beginning teachers do this by developing skills in the red quadrant, or structural domain. In the second half of this chapter, we describe Aaron's journey beyond his starting point in the red quadrant. As he opened his mind to new possibilities, he crossed the red boundary and began to integrate this perspective with the other three dimensions of the Connect Framework. In doing so his practice became more powerful.

Building Capacity in the Red Quadrant

At the start of the school year, teachers face the challenge of establishing routines (red quadrant) and building relationships (yellow quadrant) with new groups of students. In other words, at the start of the year teachers tend to be preoccupied with the internal workings of the classroom, which are represented by the left half of the Connect Framework. As we will see in Aaron's story, one of his first steps as a new teacher was to build skills in the red quadrant.

Aaron was an honor student in high school and college, but he taught remedial math to at-risk high school juniors and seniors in his first year of teaching. Unlike Aaron these students had little prior success and seemingly little desire to learn mathematics. To complicate things further, Aaron was nearly the same age as his students. As a first-year teacher, he did not have the experience and the tools to effectively manage students. In Aaron's words, "It was a really rough year."

It is common for new teachers to struggle as they begin their careers. More than 30 percent of all teachers leave the profession by the end of their fifth year.[1] The reasons they cite for leaving often include feeling overwhelmed by expectations, feeling isolated, and a lack of support.[2]

The first time Aaron was ever totally in charge of a group of students was the first day he walked into his own classroom. Unlike his pre-service teacher-training experience, there was no one in the room providing advice on how to respond to the circumstances he faced.

As is the case with many new teachers, Aaron particularly struggled with the red quadrant problem of classroom management. As a teacher, he believed he "deserved their respect and attention." When students misbehaved, Aaron knew he was "well within [his] rights to issue punishment, whether it be detentions, parent phone calls, or office referrals." Fortunately, a concerned administrator took an interest in him and helped him develop the skills he needed to successfully perform in the red quadrant. He said, "My administrator asked what the goal of all this discipline was. I answered, 'To change behavior.' She then pointed out that I did have the authority to administer discipline, but it was pointless to do so if it didn't change the student's behavior. Instead of focusing on demonstrating my authority, I should focus on ideas that would change student behavior. That changed my life."

This administrator went on to coach him on building routines and paid attention to the circumstances that contributed to the conflict Aaron was experiencing. She helped him see alternatives that would improve the outcomes of his interactions with students. With the administrator's help, Aaron found his capacity for classroom management improving. Had this improvement not occurred, he may have decided to leave the profession.

Getting Stuck in a Single Quadrant of the Framework

Once Aaron developed a set of classroom management skills, the red quadrant emerged as an area of strength, and he became more effective. When teachers learn to "manage" their classrooms, they learn how to bring some degree of structure and order to their work.

When a teacher such as Aaron develops skills associated with a particular quadrant, a more elaborate theory of practice unfolds. This is a step forward for any teacher, but it also represents a risk. A teacher who develops skills in one quadrant may end up overemphasizing the perspective and the skills associated with that quadrant. In the case of the red quadrant, the danger is establishing a classroom that is overmanaged, overstructured, and overly dependent on rules. At the extreme, a red-centered classroom can feel like a prison. Given this risk, the next step for a teacher is to stretch out of his or her comfort zone and integrate the other aspects of effectiveness. Sometimes making such a change requires a life jolt.

A Life Jolt

For Aaron a life jolt became the impetus for his commitment to begin stretching beyond his comfort zone in the red quadrant: "I always felt as though my pedagogy was strong. I had a strong math background. But learning those social elements [yellow quadrant] was much more painful for me along the way and much more challenging."

To elaborate, Aaron told us a particularly poignant story about a student, Joe, who displayed a lot of negative behaviors in class: "As a new teacher, I was struggling with ways to manage that behavior, and I wasn't being very successful. So I really stepped up my discipline with that particular student, and he began to comply. I was very proud of myself for having achieved this compliance. For me that felt like a big growth in my classroom…because I had gotten control of that student to a point of stasis where at least he wasn't bothering me and I wasn't bothering him."

Aaron had turned conflict into compliance, and his confidence in his ability to manage student behavior grew. But his growing satisfaction with his practice was cut short. On the last day of class, Aaron received a note from Joe. In the note Joe thanked Aaron for teaching him and apologized for his behavior during the school year. Joe closed the note with a sentence that shattered Aaron's newly gained confidence: "I want to let you know that I have a sister who is coming to your class next year…. Please don't give up on her the way you gave up on me."

The note drove Aaron to reexamine his most basic assumptions about self, students, teaching, and learning. In reflecting on the impact of this event, Aaron shared how his perspective changed: "It forces you to step back and think of what it is you do and how it is you treat your students and how you are perceived. I had become so focused on gaining control of this student that I damaged him as a person. He hadn't achieved academically; he hadn't grown and developed. We had reached a stasis, and in education stasis isn't good enough. He deserved my best every day, just like every other student."

Such lessons open the mind by jolting our orientation to our work. *Life jolts* tend to challenge your assumptions and alter your perspective. Aaron told us that this painful lesson is something that he continues to carry with him: "It's been a dozen years ago that this has happened, and these kinds of stories stay with you as reminders."

Aaron's story is an example of the developmental plateaus we all experience in life. Once teachers find their comfort zone, they are often confronted with situations for which that notion of teaching is inadequate. What Aaron had initially defined as success was redefined as a new challenge. To continue to grow as a teacher and reach every student, he had to stretch his practice. He had to build skills in other areas—in particular the yellow quadrant.

TEACHER'S TIP

Aaron: My success in the red quadrant came by improving my ability in the yellow quadrant. I was so focused on management that I neglected to build relationships with my students. This undermined my success in the red quadrant. Classroom management needs to be coupled with a connection to students. Find a colleague whom you trust, give him or her a copy of the Connect Framework, and ask that he or she observe your teaching. Ask him or her to reflect with you on your strengths and ask about areas in which you can improve. You may be surprised. Sometimes the area that you feel you need to grow in is not the real problem at all.

Deep Change and the Developmental Process

Aaron's story illustrates the process of deep change. As described in chapter 1, deep change is a process of transformative learning. A life jolt can lead you to examine your existing assumptions and formulate new ones. Once Aaron read the note from Joe, he could never look at his teaching in the same way. Like Kelli, he had to learn new ways to be with students.

RESEARCH FOUNDATIONS

Developmental Change

Robert Kegan, an authority on adult development, talks about deep change as "developmental change." His work is important because it recognizes that transformative learning occurs throughout a person's life rather than just in the "formative" years.[3]

In his writing Kegan examines two aspects of the developmental process that on the surface seem contradictory. On the one hand, most people go through developmental changes over the course of their lifetimes. During these shifts, people fundamentally alter their ways of making meaning. Because meaning-making is central to our concepts of identity, these kinds of shifts often result in changes in how people understand themselves and the world around them.

The process of development, however is also characterized by periods of stability in which there is very little change in how we construct meaning. Some level of stability is desirable because it allows us to more consistently make judgments and take action. But Kegan notes a downside to stability. Over time it produces a kind of "immunity to change."[4] Comfort, order, and predictability are inherently easier to manage than novelty, disruption, and change.

When you make sense of things in a particular way over a long period of time, you are less likely to see and value alternative perspectives. Many of the "isms" that characterize the world—sexism, racism, ageism, tribalism—are a result of individuals or groups becoming too comfortable with a limited way of making meaning. When you get stuck in one of these patterns, as Aaron did early in his career, you can unwittingly become stuck in your old assumptions.

This aspect of Kegan's work helps us better understand the challenges associated with deep change. Even relatively simple kinds of change—things like losing weight, exercising more, or becoming more assertive—are often difficult to accomplish because of the particular immunities to change that we build up over time.

> The challenge becomes to maintain some level of stability while remaining open and receptive to the prospect of deepening, widening, and, in some cases, reconstructing your perspective. When we refer to teachers who are engaged in *continuous improvement,* we are talking about their capacity to remain open and receptive to the deepening and widening of a particular perspective. Change and stability are both important to development and how we learn to engage the world.

After Aaron read the note from Joe, he realized that being in control is not the same thing as being effective. He began to see the unanticipated negative repercussions of his classroom management strategies. Joe became compliant, but he also did not achieve academically. Deep change takes place when the limitations of the old perspective become apparent. Through this encounter Aaron realized that he had to work harder on developing relational skills (yellow quadrant).

To go through this kind of realization and change is neither easy nor straightforward. More often than not, it requires long periods of personal reflection, multiple interactions with colleagues and friends, and probably many sleepless nights. After all, this kind of development is about changing our relationship with ideas that previously defined us. It is like putting away a map that we depended on, finding a new map that is both unfamiliar and untested, and then working from that map to move forward. Deep change is not simple and it is not comfortable, but it is life altering.

Kelli's response to the suggestion that she was not "the key to every door" is another example of this kind of developmental shift. Kelli redefined how she would interact with students, especially difficult ones, and how she would make meaning of her work. What is missing from her story in chapter 1 is the real work she had to do to develop her new perspective. It is serious work that has consequences for oneself, one's students, and one's relationships with colleagues. This is why, in many cases, some kind of existential crisis is often necessary to trigger this kind of shift. Deep change is difficult to undertake, and if the stakes are not high enough, we may understandably choose to back away. This may be why a life jolt is often necessary to get us into the deep change process. Transformative learning is inherently difficult.

Working across the Quadrant Boundaries

Development does not follow a straight-line trajectory. Aaron did a lot of work in the red quadrant. He then recognized a need to stretch his practice into the yellow quadrant. Other teachers may begin in different places and move in different directions. But whatever path they take, it seems that HETs are engaged in the continual integration of the quadrants. As discussed in chapter 2, we call this kind of integration *powerful practice* to denote the heightened levels of effectiveness that are available when the different dimensions of effectiveness are integrated.

Aaron is now less constrained by the boundaries of the four quadrants. Each quadrant is an aspect of life and of teaching that Aaron honors. He moves easily within the quadrants, but he also moves across them. This integration can be seen in Aaron's comments about control: "You are allotted a certain amount of control by your role as the teacher, and you can use that control in a lot of ways" (red quadrant). Some teachers go too far, and control becomes oppressive. Others go too far in the opposite direction. They relinquish control, and the class oppresses them. Aaron takes a different path. He likes to create a context in which he guides rather than "dictates" the class. His goal is to "teach students to control themselves" rather than his having to control students. For example, Aaron occasionally arrives late to class when he is delayed by his hall duties. Like some of the other HETs we spoke with, Aaron indicates that his students are able to start without him: "I walked in the class, and they'd already started without me. To me that was a win. They knew what they were supposed to do, and they were halfway done with it before I got into the room. I've had classes where if I need to step out for a minute you just select a student, tell him to do it, and [he will] take over for you."

Aaron knows how to set expectations for students. This allows the students to internalize routines and provides them with an inherent sense of predictability.

⊘ TEACHER'S TIP

Aaron: I impose order only when I need to. I tell students, "If you can control your own behavior, there is no need for me to control it for you. Rules exist because someone before you created the need for them. For example, some teachers say, 'No gum chewing.' Why do you think that is? It is because someone before you placed their gum under a desk or on the floor and created a mess. If you conduct yourself in a way that respects other students, the custodians, and the school, the rule is unnecessary."

Like Diana, Aaron believes that his teaching is at its best when students become connected in a web (yellow quadrant) of creative interactions, when they "challenge" the teacher and "push" the teacher to the edge of his or her understanding (blue quadrant). He is also in a mode of continuous improvement (green quadrant) as he tries to figure out ways to better achieve his goals for the class.

Aaron is describing something that is hard to understand. Each quadrant in the Connect Framework is a logical category that is readily recognizable and differentiated from the others. Even a novice teacher can quickly comprehend the different facets of practice that are represented in the framework. Masterful teachers may be able to see and do more. Aaron, for example, has had his own experiences with what Diana calls the "living beast." He refers to this unusual learning dynamic as the emergence of "a very different realm."

Aaron loves when this process occurs. It often pushes him beyond what he knows while his students move to a new level and ask penetrating questions.[5] Aaron says that often he "does not know the answer." Instead of dreading this situation, he welcomes it. He says he has to then become "authentic with the students and say, 'I don't know.'" At that point the teacher and the students are equals—learning together in a way that is very real and compelling. They are in position to co-create knowledge.

Aaron: There are lots of great ways to say, "I don't know":

- "Does anyone have an idea about that?"
- "Who would like to look that up for us tonight?"
- "I'm wondering what would happen if I try..."

Try making up a few problems on the spot so that you can say, "I don't know; let's figure it out together," and then do it. This is a great way to model problem-solving strategies for students.

To get to this interaction level requires an emphasis on relevance (green quadrant). Aaron has to take his students outside the classroom— he has to "connect the students to something that they've had success with in the past or something that they can connect with on a cultural level." He says, "If I can get that hook in, either something they understand well or something that is of high interest to them,...we can create a lot of interaction, and that really is the key to a successful lesson."

From the start of the year, Aaron fosters the development of the "different realm." Doing so requires a more complex view of leading and organizing. This is particularly true around issues of control. Aaron makes some important statements about control:

- "You spend a lot of time those first few weeks allowing students to exercise that freedom appropriately, trying to evoke comments from them, evoke answers, evoke input so they realize, *Yes, we are talking here.* This is not me speaking down to you or speaking at you. For a lot of them, that's different. That's not something they're used to."

- "There are a lot of ways to maintain control in the classroom. I personally don't like to establish myself as a dictator looking over my minions, and this is my regime and you should do as I say. I like to create a context where the kids can feel free to interact, where they recognize my role and their role, but at the same time they're not afraid to contribute or to challenge or to push."

■ "You'll hear a lot of students speaking out in my class. The key [question] is: Are you speaking out about the topic and are you waiting your turn?"

When we think of teaching in terms of control, we are making assumptions of hierarchy (red quadrant). The teacher is in charge, and the students are expected to obey. This is a good thing. Yet when this is carried too far, the class feels oppressive. Aaron, who had to work so hard initially to learn the skills of classroom control, then had to learn how to share that control with students.

Aaron does not "speak down" to his students. He seeks to make students equals in the conversation. He expects students to creatively interact with him, the material, and each other, and even challenge or push him. Yet he simultaneously expects students to "recognize my role and their role." He expects them to "speak out" but also to wait their turn. The above paragraph suggests the integration of seemingly conflicting ideas. While they may be conflicting in the mind of the novice, in the mind of the master teacher they become integrated and reinforcing. Aaron has learned how to transform classroom management into a powerful practice (see figure 3.1).

Aaron's "different realm" emerges as the four quadrants interpenetrate. Hierarchy (red quadrant) is minimized but does not go away. It becomes dormant as a community of equals (yellow quadrant) becomes a community of creative inquiry (green quadrant) in pursuit of a challenging purpose (blue quadrant). Note that while Aaron expects his students to operate out of the yellow, green, and blue quadrants, he also wants them to be able to flip back into the red hierarchy as necessary. He expects them to move back and forth between and across the quadrants as the activity dictates. He is teaching his students to integrate the four quadrants—to engage in powerful practice.

While development can change your original perspective, it does not negate it. Powerful practice is not about giving up your core identity as a teacher. When we look at Aaron today, we see a teacher who remains

Figure 3.1 *Classroom Management as a Powerful Practice*

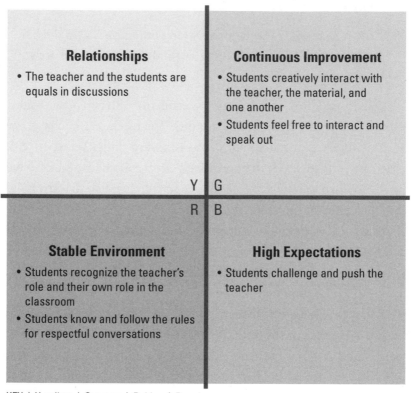

Relationships

- The teacher and the students are equals in discussions

Continuous Improvement

- Students creatively interact with the teacher, the material, and one another
- Students feel free to interact and speak out

Y | G

R | B

Stable Environment

- Students recognize the teacher's role and their own role in the classroom
- Students know and follow the rules for respectful conversations

High Expectations

- Students challenge and push the teacher

KEY | Y: yellow | G: green | B: blue | R: red

very comfortable and strong in the red quadrant. When Aaron's assumptions about effective teaching were challenged, he opened his mind to incorporating aspects of effective practice that were not active before. There is a developmental pattern here. The attributes of each quadrant begin to reinforce rather than compete with one another.

For example, when teachers begin to integrate the red quadrant with the attributes of the other three quadrants, the structures and the processes in the red quadrant begin to serve different purposes. When the red attributes are integrated with the yellow quadrant, structures and processes are viewed as ways to enhance the nature and the quality of relationships in the classroom. When the red quadrant is integrated with the blue quadrant, structures and processes are viewed as ways to broaden and deepen students' academic achievement. When the red quadrant is integrated with the green quadrant, structures and processes are viewed as ways to set boundaries within which creative thought can emerge. Teachers who have achieved this level of integration in the classroom may be less likely to discuss classroom management in terms of classroom control. For these teachers control may become an aspect of their practice on which they seldom need to focus. Order occurs as a naturally emergent aspect of the educational process because students want to be orderly.

Stretching from the Red Quadrant

The red quadrant is important to every teacher because effective structures provide more time for teaching and learning. Students need a sense of order and discipline; they need to know how to organize their work and "what to expect." One of our HETs told us, for example, "You have your classrooms set up so that you're not involved in the smaller tasks. You have to be involved in the learning, the teaching. I don't want to know if someone's pencil got broken. They have a procedure for that."

TEACHER'S TIP

Aaron: Too many rules or procedures create confusion for students. Rules should be simple and easy to understand. Their purpose is to ensure an environment that is safe and fair. For example:

- Be prompt.
- Be prepared.
- Be polite.

Rules are much easier to follow when they make sense. If you can't offer a sound reason for why you have a rule, perhaps you shouldn't have it.

Routines should be procedural and are meant to ensure smooth transitions. They should flow logically from desired outcomes. For example: "When you are done with your paper, it should go here so that I can find it" or "We sharpen our pencil before class so we don't have to interrupt the lesson."

Not all HETs approach the red quadrant in the same way. Some of our interviewees spoke of setting rules in a direct fashion, whereas others spoke of involving students (yellow quadrant) in the development of rules. Still others spoke of moving beyond rules to a more complex kind of order, or the "different realm." Most, like Aaron, are masters of crossing boundaries and integrating categories. Here we consider some of the themes associated with integrating the red quadrant with others (see figure 3.2).

Figure 3.2 *Stretching from the Red Quadrant*

	Directive Perspective	**Co-creative Perspective**
Role of student	Follower	Leader
Peer pressure	Negative	Positive
Order	Imposed order	Emergent order
Content	Prescribed	Customized

Role of the Student: Follower versus Leader

From the perspective of the red quadrant, rules and routines are necessary for smooth functioning. In a conventional hierarchy, it is standard to assume that order is something a teacher imposes on students. The teacher is the leader and the students are followers. The danger, however, is that too much order may lead to boredom and stagnation. As a teacher becomes more masterful, he or she may tend to view structures in a more complex way. Aaron, for example, says, "I think a lot of times we tend to throw out blanket rules without having a reason behind them. It's one thing to tell students, 'Oh, you shouldn't talk.' It's another thing to say, 'So-and-so is talking. Wait your turn.' You're teaching a different lesson there."

Aaron is suggesting that structure is not his purpose. Structure serves his purpose. Structure does not just emerge by setting rules—it also is shaped in minute-to-minute interactions.

TEACHER'S TIP

Aaron: When I talk to a pre-service teacher, I emphasize the difference between walking into a classroom and trying to convince the students you are in charge and walking into a classroom knowing you are in charge. The first teacher feels that he or she has something to prove and works to impose order. The second has nothing to prove and order emerges on its own.

Teachers like Aaron have complex expectations. They want students to operate in an orderly fashion while also taking initiative. They want students to be leaders of learning. Rules thus become a means to ensure that students know how to appropriately engage in their own learning. The desire is for students to internalize the procedures while taking responsibility for what goes on in the classroom.

Aaron told us that the internalization of routines frees both the students and the teacher. This is a complex notion. Structure and control are paths to freedom and learning. Other HETs whom we interviewed also illustrated this point:

- "Structure and routine are there so they [students] can work outside the box."

- "I think the more structured and organized I am, the more creative we can be. Without structure it doesn't work. We need organized chaos. We need some way to manage the mess. Structure and order free me."

Appropriate boundaries help teachers and students channel their energy toward the desired outcomes.

Peer Pressure: Negative versus Positive

Peer pressure in schools is often negative; it tends to constrict performance. When peer pressure is transformed, it creates a new dynamic. Instead of seeking ways to disrupt, students embrace the common good and do what is right because they are part of a learning community. It becomes not only acceptable but also necessary to do the right thing. This minimizes the normal policing role that many teachers play and frees the teacher to focus on other things.

One of the HETs we interviewed described the transformation of peer pressure and then made an interesting claim illustrating the power of intrinsic motivation: "The social pressure is positive. In our class we are all working for the common good. My kids walk down the hall in a different way. They willingly stay in line. There is no need for external pressure. They take personal ownership."

Another teacher made a similar claim: "I don't have to tell my kids to be quiet in the hallway. I don't have to tell them to be respectful during assembly. No one likes to be bossed around or given rules. I don't have any rules in my classroom. Just be respectful. If you can't be respectful, then I'll have to create rules."

The transformation of peer pressure is an important change. It is a powerful version of structure that forms shared values (yellow quadrant) and frees the teacher (green quadrant) while increasing the likelihood of student success (blue quadrant).

At one HET workshop, a teacher explained how he facilitates this process. He said it is critical to get students on your side, to turn the class into a "team." He told the story of a boy named Sam. One day during class, he told his students that he was going to play a very serious song, and he did not want them to laugh. The teacher actually played a funny song, and students laughed. At that point Sam stood up and called his classmates out. He told them that the teacher told them not to laugh.

The incident was not planned, but the teacher indicated that it was very important—the very thing he needed to start happening: "I knew at that moment that I've got this one. I'm going to be able to effect some change with this child in this year because I knew he was on my side and he understood that I was on his side."

The teacher explained that he needed the "kids to stand behind him" just as they needed to know that he would "stand behind them."

Order: Imposed versus Emergent

In one of our interviews, a teacher talked at length about her focus on discipline. When the topic of order emerged, the interviewer asked about rules. She replied, "I do not have rules." We asked how this was possible. She responded:

> I let them know a little bit about myself on a personal level so that they understand that I'm first a person and not some robot teacher up in front of their classroom. And then I get to know them a little bit in a personal way. I excuse their weaknesses for the first two to three weeks....I let them be third graders. While I'm building to this focus and this seriousness, for the first little bit, I'm allowing them to learn. I treat them with the tenderness and care to let them know I understand where you are, but [misbehaviors] are not going to be accepted in this classroom. I build up almost a parent relationship with the kids....I set up the consequences, but there are few rules. My kids are allowed to get up and use the restroom whenever they want. I don't even have a bathroom policy. I find that my kids don't get up and go to the bathroom all the time because they are afraid they'll miss something in the class.

This teacher went on to say, "In my words, in my looks, in my actions, they know that I mean business." So she uses body language to convey the blue quadrant message that learning is a serious business while using intimacy and tolerance to establish yellow quadrant relationships. As caring and trust increase (yellow quadrant), she also clarifies expectations for conduct (red quadrant) and performance (blue quadrant). Order does not come from establishing rules; it emerges through interaction.

Her last sentence is particularly interesting. While students are free to go to the bathroom at any time, few go because what she does is so engaging that they prefer to be in the classroom. Instead of using the power of coercion, she is using the power of attraction to keep her students grounded in the classroom experience.

Content: Prescribed versus Customized

Another example of stretching outside the red quadrant has to do with the customization of required material. Content is usually prescribed by the district or state in which one teaches (blue quadrant). It may or may not fit the needs and the interests of a given class, and this can be a source of frustration. As a teacher becomes more masterful, however, he or she may develop the skill to transform content, to make it more relevant and meaningful (green quadrant).

- ■ "They [students] don't care to learn something that doesn't seem to have any place in their lives. I have to really make it relevant for them to be interested."

- ■ "Unfortunately, in school we can't teach every kid individually what they're most interested in because there are some things they need to learn whether they think they need to learn it or not. They've got to get that background. So, I think one of the things, as a teacher, I should be trying to show them is *why* they need to learn that, or give them a reason for it, or try to put that little enticing thing into it, you know, the game or that something that will make them not even realize they're learning. They're learning in spite of everything else."

One of the many tools for making material relevant is the use of personal stories. Stories are powerful mechanisms to help students make a connection with the concepts being taught. An HET told us that she spends a great deal of time thinking about stories she can use to make learning relevant:

> I drive to work, and whenever you have free time you think—what is a story that would take this content and make it mean something to the kids? You know if you're talking about predators or scavengers, I talk about the road-kill I see on the side of the road going to work.... So the kids are there. They've all seen it, you know, and so now they know that those things that are picking that deer or whatever, those are the scavengers. That means something now, not just the word *scavengers*. So the next time they see it, which they will, you know it clicks. You try to think of ways you can make it mean something to an 11-year-old kid....At the end of every year, I ask them what helped them learn the most in my room, and they'll always say, "The stories you tell." Kids love to listen to stories, and it's almost like they must place themselves in that as a character in that story.

TEACHER'S TIP

Aaron: Nothing improves a lesson like adding a narrative. When I have a particularly difficult lesson, I sometimes stop and ask the class, "Can I tell you a story?" You can see the level of anxiety drop in the room. Two boats traveling upstream at different rates is far less interesting than a canoe full of tourists being chased by a canoe full of cannibals. A story about *my* dog (with a picture included) is way better than a problem about "a dog."

In a workshop discussion about making learning relevant, one HET gave a warning: "Don't try to be someone you're not. You may want to be like that great teacher down the hall, but if you put on a face that isn't consistent with who you are on the inside, the kids will sense it and it won't work." Parker Palmer talks about teaching as a "presentation of self."[6] The question *Who will I be with my students?* is pivotal for teachers, especially those who are early in their careers. Until teachers figure this out, they are working at teaching rather than *being* a teacher. Until they become self-defining, self-empowering, and self-accountable, they are stuck doing what they think they should be doing as opposed to acting authentically.

Authenticity is important. This is illustrated through another story shared by one of our interviewees. She is a very serious teacher. She was told that she was required to have a Halloween party. She felt the party was a disruption to her plan, so she turned the party into a science class. This unusual strategy may sound like a recipe for disaster, but the students said it was "the best party ever."

Faced with the rules of the school, the teacher accepted them (red quadrant) but became creative (green quadrant). She maintained her focus on performance (blue quadrant) and made it work because it was authentic. By integrating the four quadrants, she became the best teacher she could be.

Summary

In this chapter we described the process of development using the red quadrant as a starting point. Aaron's story illustrates that it is important to become skilled in the red quadrant, and it is also important to stretch across the red boundary. As Alda suggests in the epigraph, the assumptions that Aaron makes about the students and the classroom become his "windows on the world." As Aaron broadened his perspective to include the other quadrants of the Connect Framework, his ideas about teaching and learning became more complex. As you become more complex, you also become more capable.

PLANTING SEEDS

1. Aaron could not effectively manage a classroom. Then he acquired a mentor who taught him the key skills of classroom management. She analyzed specific interactions between Aaron and his students and helped him see alternatives that improved his ability to manage his interactions with students. Who has played a significant role in your development as a teacher? How can you continue to make connections with people who can help you stretch and grow?

2. Aaron's goal is to "teach students to control themselves" rather than his having to control students. Students internalize the routines, and there is an internalized sense of predictability. Aaron, for example, is sometimes delayed in hall duties and is late to class. Like some of the other HETs, Aaron indicates that the students then start without him. If you were late, would your students start without you? What does it take for such a thing to happen?

3. Aaron likes to create a context in which he guides rather than "dictates" the class. He believes that some teachers go too far, and control becomes oppressive. Others relinquish control, and the class oppresses them. Aaron believes that his teaching is at its best when students become connected in a web of creative interactions, when students "challenge" the teacher and "push" the teacher to the edge of the teacher's understanding. Aaron describes the creation of this kind of interaction as the emergence of "a very different realm." What is the ideal point between

oppression and relinquishing control? What is the "different realm" that emerges at this ideal point?

4. Aaron's "different realm" emerges as the four quadrants interpenetrate. Hierarchy (red quadrant) is minimized but does not go away. It becomes dormant as a community of equals (yellow quadrant) becomes a community of creative inquiry (green quadrant) in pursuit of a challenging purpose (blue quadrant). Note that while Aaron expects his students to operate out of the yellow, green, and blue quadrants, he also wants them to be able to flip back into the red hierarchy as necessary. He expects them to move back and forth between and across the quadrants as the activity dictates. What does it mean for a teacher to cross categories and to help students cross categories? Why is this a key to entering the different realm or the emergence of the living beast?

GROWING YOUR PRACTICE

1. Reevaluate the rules and the procedures that you have established for your classroom. Should any be dropped, changed, or added? Is the purpose of each rule and procedure clear to your students? Consider inviting your students to help you define what will make your classroom a successful learning environment.

2. Which quadrant is your strong suit? Identify one practice that would help you stretch authentically from your area of strength into each of the other three quadrants. Try one new practice in the coming week.

CHAPTER 4

Opening the Heart:
Enhancing Relationships

One looks back with appreciation to the brilliant teachers, but with gratitude to those who touched our human feeling. The curriculum is so much necessary raw material, but warmth is the vital element for the growing plant and for the soul of the child.

—Carl Jung
The Gifted Child

SARAH IS A HIGH SCHOOL ENGLISH TEACHER. SHE HAS SEVEN YEARS of experience, yet she speaks with the wisdom of someone who has been teaching for 30. Since the beginning of her career, she has taught in a large urban district. She knows her content well but, as Jung suggests in the epigraph, her content is just the "necessary raw material." It is an excuse to form relationships that grow children. She is particularly aware of the students who have been damaged by life.

In speaking about her practice, Sarah often uses the word *mediation*. She sees herself as a facilitator and a catalyst, someone who, like Diana, makes connections so that new things happen. Her most immediate concern is how to negotiate the rift between the content she must teach and the real-life experiences of her students.

She loves to teach English because in English "you get to talk about everything." For Sarah this includes authentic conversations that engage both her and her students: "We talk about a lot of things that have fear associated with them, and we talk about them openly. And things sometimes get a little bit heated. I might cry—not because I'm mad at them but because the conversation is so moving."

Sarah also finds herself processing her own experiences through her students' needs to talk about and work through difficult social issues. One of Sarah's favorite books to teach is *The House on Mango Street* because it confronts many of the issues that are real to her students. "There is an amazing amount [of] class stuff, gender stuff, sexual abuse....There [are] just all these things that come up." While discussing such issues, Sarah sees a need to be authentic and vulnerable. She is always asking herself, *Am I going to be willing to talk about these things openly, both experiences that I've had and also to say, "I don't have any experience with that"?*

Sarah believes that it is essential to have these conversations because she often feels like students are passive observers of their education because the directive perspective is taken too far. She feels that overly directive teaching can minimize the emotional content of the curriculum. Rather than tell her students what is right or wrong, she wants them to engage and "negotiate" difficult social issues so that they come to their own deep understanding of what is right and wrong.

Like other HETs, Sarah focuses on continuously improving as a teacher. For Sarah teaching is a "multilayered process." As she works to peel back the layers of the content and her students' experiences with it, she continually expands and deepens her understanding of what it means to be an effective teacher. The process engages both her mind and her emotions. Sarah believes that new possibilities emerge when she opens her heart.

CHAPTER OVERVIEW

Opening the Heart

Chapter 4 explores the benefits and the challenges associated with teaching from the heart. We discover how Sarah and other HETs use their strengths in the yellow quadrant of the Connect Framework to build communities of learning that include even those students who have disengaged from school. Sarah creates a high-functioning classroom culture to nurture collective learning. We see how learning is accelerated by teachers who touch "our human feeling," beginning with a lesson from early in Sarah's career.

Building Capacity in the Yellow Quadrant

In her first year, Sarah taught at "a pretty tough high school." Like Aaron in chapter 3, she found it difficult to connect with her students (yellow quadrant) and to successfully manage her classroom (red quadrant). Many of these issues stemmed from the directive assumptions Sarah carried into her first job. She believed that her job was to become an expert in her subject matter and to transfer that knowledge to her students (red quadrant skills). She told us, "When I started teaching, I was so focused on and worried about my curriculum, my books, and my writing products...that the child was this vehicle through which I was going to show that I was a good teacher."

Early on Sarah also believed that her passion for reading, writing, and literature would automatically carry over to her students. She found that this was not the case. Halfway through her first quarter, Sarah described herself as "crying a lot."

Like Aaron, Sarah was overwhelmed by her inability to be the teacher she thought she was supposed to be. Her students were uncooperative, and they were not learning very much. In desperation she reached out to her principal and confided her fears: "I'm doing it all wrong, and I think I'm actually damaging them [students]."

From Teacher-Centered to Student-Centered

Fortunately, Sarah had a savvy and supportive principal, whose advice was not about technique but about perspective. The principal told Sarah, "Stop looking at your own teaching. Start really looking at and listening to your kids. They will let you know what they need....Stop being the bird who is squawking all the time. Be the observing bird and be quiet and listen more, and really look at your students and look at their writing and look at what they're doing. They're telling you very clearly what is working and what is not."

When Sarah speaks of this advice, she does so with a deep sense of admiration and appreciation. It led to a personal transformation: "What I saw [in my teaching] was that I was just kind of presenting stuff in a language that was familiar to me and a language that worked for me, and

I wasn't really presenting it in a way that had anything to do with the kids and what they were interested in."

With a better understanding of why she was not being successful, Sarah began to move beyond the directive mode toward a more generative kind of teaching. This move felt natural for her because of the empathy she already felt for her students. Like many of her students, Sarah grew up in a troubled home and—in contrast with many of the HETs we interviewed—she had not seen school as a safe haven away from these circumstances. Sarah recalls, "I was awful in high school. I was constantly suspended. I was constantly in trouble. I hated school. I thought it was a load of crap."

Despite the difficulties she experienced at home and in school, Sarah also recognizes that she had the resources she needed to grapple with her circumstances as a teenager: "I always had a roof over my head. I always had food. I was always clothed....There was this older woman who lived across the street, and I went to her house like every day—I lived there. I read to her. She read to me. You know, I had resources."

Sarah now views her work with high school students as a kind of advocacy: "As I'm advocating for kids that were my age, I'm also kind of healing myself by…advocating for myself in a way."

Even today Sarah sometimes finds herself slipping back into a narrow focus on content. When this happens she reminds herself of the advice she received from her principal: "The most important thing is the kids and what they're actually trying to tell me at that moment and how they're trying to communicate what they need via behavior, via actually speaking it, whether directly or indirectly."

We heard similar stories from other HETs who are able to draw on difficult personal experiences to authentically empathize with their students. One HET shared the profound learning that grew out of the death of one of her children:

> I think that there's a certain kindness that develops because of a death of a child and a certain caring and sweetness. You realize that life is not forever. You realize that every life is precious....I think that's probably the most defining characteristic of my life. [It] probably brought about a lot of changes in who I was as a person, brought

about a lot of the softness that I feel toward children, toward human-kind totally, because you never know what people are going through until you really get involved in their lives. And I think even like the little girl [in my classroom] whose mother is in prison, and she had to go live with her grandmother this year. I think about how difficult that had to be for that little girl, even though her life with her mother was horrible. I think that little girl must be so traumatized by life and that I too was traumatized at one point. And I realized how being in the corner, cowering like a kitten, is probably what I wanted to do—so I think I have that empathy because of that defining moment.

Another HET described how her divorce changed who she was as a teacher: "I've been able to experience some difficulties in my life that I think helped me identify with some of my students in a way that I might not have. I look at other teachers who have not experienced some of these things and think maybe it's more difficult for them to understand and empathize with the students."

The same teacher went on to talk about her divorce and the effect it had on her and her three children. She spoke of her own pain as well as the responsibility she felt for helping her children with their pain. These experiences brought a new perspective to her teaching:

And I think it really helps me to have some insight....And you know, I think that the more you've experienced, the more you can empathize and understand other people's situations. So the kids that come to school and don't have a dad or they don't have a mom, I understand a little bit more the pain that they're going through, the struggle that they have to feel working every day, just by watching my own children go through the pain of not having a dad that cares about them.

These are poignant stories, but everyone experiences adversity. Adversity can take many forms, such as illness, caregiving, and loneliness. In working through these challenges, we often grow in surprising and unexpected ways. Post-traumatic growth is a form of learning from adversity that can give rise to many positive characteristics, including empathy.[1] Having experienced this kind of deep change, some teachers, like Sarah, emerge with new ways of making sense of the world that better equip them to help students make the deep changes that are necessary for their continuing development. Yet to help students do this requires more than empathy.

⬤ *TEACHER'S TIP*

Sarah: I believe that teachers have to be well emotionally. I have to take good care of myself emotionally, physically, spiritually, and intellectually so that I can help my kids and so that I can empower my kids to do that for themselves too. It is not about any one discipline; it is a way of life.

From Student-Centered to Learning-Centered

In our conversations with Sarah about the evolution of her practice, she first spoke of improving her effectiveness by paying more attention to the needs of her students (yellow quadrant). But empathy alone does not make teachers effective; there are pitfalls associated with empathetic practice. Teachers can become so mired in their students' problems that they are unable to engage those same students academically. Sarah indicates that her capacity to deal with this tension comes from the "hard work" she had to do as a teenager and as a young adult: "I had a messed-up childhood, and I made a lot of poor choices early in life, and in order to break that cycle you've got to do the hard work. You've got to get really real with yourself, really honest with yourself. I don't think many people in general do that or want to do that. I think there are people that do, but it's hard."

Sarah constantly struggles to balance empathy (yellow quadrant) with challenging her students (blue quadrant) to do the hard work they need to do to transcend their current circumstances. She describes a typical inner struggle: "Do I do the tough love and draw the hard line? Is that what's best for this kid, or do we do one more chance? That is the struggle. Sometimes I honestly just don't know."

The capacity to integrate the yellow and blue quadrants is crucial to developing a learning-centered orientation. People who teach by opening their heart must guard against developing co-dependent relationships with their students. When empathy overshadows learning, the relationship can exacerbate the issue rather than help the student move through it. Ultimately, this kind of relationship serves neither the teacher nor the student. Sarah speaks of her capacity to avoid this trap: "A lot of my students are up against enormous obstacles—way bigger than what I had—but I also know that feeling of *I don't care; you don't care; nobody cares; why am I even trying?* So because I've been there, I think I also will not let that become an excuse. A lot of my kids, they'll tell me something and I'm like, 'That is an explanation, absolutely. That totally explains why you slept in my class, but it doesn't excuse it. It's not okay with me.'"

As Sarah empathizes with her students, she also teaches them blue quadrant skills such as "how to advocate for themselves and get resources for themselves." Sarah explains to her students that these are skills they will need for the rest of their lives. She wants her students to be able to articulate their needs and find resources to meet those needs: "If you are that tired, just let me know. I'm going to let you go sleep in the nurse's office. I'm not out to get you, but this is the way the world works. You've got to communicate your needs really, really clearly, and then the other person is going to say, *This is what I can or cannot do to meet your needs.* And then you get to make your decision accordingly."

Sarah speaks openly with her students about why she has such high expectations for them: "I cry with them about their hardships and stuff [and tell them], 'Because you are up against all these things, that's why you need to do well in my class. Because you have all these things going on in your life is why you'd better be damned sure you can write and read and speak. Because those are free for you right now, and they are the most valuable tools you will ever have in your life, period.'"

✎ *TEACHER'S TIP*

Sarah: Having a choice matters to students. Students tell me that that is when they are most invested or intrinsically motivated. But there are times when I feel like I know what is best, so I don't give them a choice. Sometimes I need to push them in a particular direction because I know it is going to help them grow or it is going to benefit them. For example, I may say, "I want you to know this particular cultural reference because when you go to college and you are sitting in a lecture hall, you will hear it again. I want that bell to go off so that you feel like you belong in college."

Some HETs told stories of growing up in poverty or in abusive families. In the process of moving forward, they talked about how particular experiences altered their assumptions of who they were, who they could be, and what they could do. In some cases friends, family, or mentors helped them through these challenges, but in other cases these teachers simply found the strength and the courage to face the challenge themselves. Like Sarah they learned their way into a new perspective. One HET commented, "Growing up I had nothing, so I *know* how these kids are. I have a lot of kids who are from low economic situations. I made it and you can make it. You have potential. You're going to use it."

This quote suggests another factor that may help teachers shift from student-centered teaching to learning-centered teaching. Persevering through tough circumstances can lead people to discover potential they did not know they had. This discovery may enable them to more readily see the potential in others. Because these teachers have learned their way through tough circumstances, they also *know* that their students can do the same. Perhaps teachers who have worked through adversity are better able to integrate the yellow and blue quadrants, that is, to recognize the need to challenge their students while also supporting them.

TEACHER'S TIP

Sarah: To be present means to be still, to be quiet, to look, to listen, and to remember to breathe. I know that sounds really simple, but that is hard for me to do. For example, we talk about wait time. Two years ago I looked at, not just the wait time after I asked a question but also the wait time after a student responded and then I responded or another student responded. It was like nil. My need to immediately keep the lesson moving forward was preventing me from allowing 30 seconds pass to let a concept sink in or to give students and myself time to really think about what was just said. That is tough, but it is important.

Building a High-Functioning Culture

The yellow quadrant has a collective orientation. Collaborative learning happens in a network of trusting relationships, not just between the teacher and her students but also among the students themselves. Sarah regularly works to build trust and open communication in her classroom. She shared a prime example.

A senior at her high school committed suicide, and everyone was shocked and saddened. The student had shown no signs of being in distress. "This kid was really happy, very nice, just an extremely well-liked and helpful kid."

Sarah learned of the student's death on Saturday, and she spent the rest of the weekend agonizing over how to address the tragedy on Monday. She knew that her students might want and need to talk about what they were thinking and feeling, but she was not sure how to engage them in conversation. On the other hand, her students might prefer to avoid the subject completely. She designed a lesson plan for the day and went into the classroom that morning prepared to "read" her students and to be open to their needs. As her students entered the classroom, she could see that some had been crying and some were still crying. Sarah described what happened next: "I was just in front of the class, and I started crying. And then this girl said, 'Why are you crying?' And I just said, 'I'm sad because you're hurting. I hurt because you hurt.' Then we all just started talking about what happened [and] how we felt about what happened."

Sarah concluded this story by going in a very different direction. She talked about her students' courage, their capacity to transcend these kinds of experiences, and how she feels privileged to be allowed into their world. Sarah's classroom culture encourages students to share themselves in a personal way, and when this happens these experiences feel "sacred." Sarah said, "Kids will write you just normal teenage stuff—'I am lonely; I don't feel like anyone likes me; I feel fat'—you know, stuff that we say to ourselves in our interior monologue every day. But their willingness to be vulnerable and share it with the group is just—it's humbling. So I try to make space for that and let them know that it's safe here."

When we asked her to say a little more about why these kinds of experiences are humbling, she began to tear up as she told us, "When you give them [students] just a little trust, a little bit of yourself, a little bit of love, and a little bit of hard work, they respond tenfold, and a lot of times I just don't feel deserving....It's humbling because it's an honor to get to see that part of someone.

It may be that this kind of openness and trust plays an important role in the emergence of a culture in which learning accelerates and lives change.

⬤ *TEACHER'S TIP*

Sarah: Every once in a while, we get in a big circle, and students are allowed to read anything that they have written. They can pass too. Little things like this let them know that I get it—you are exposed to *this, this,* and *this.* There is no bad; there is no good; there is no right; there is no wrong. We pay attention to our actions and our feelings when these kinds of things come up, and then we have a conversation. "Is my reaction the same as yours?" "Why not?" I think so many times we get scared when dicey conversations come up, and maybe rightfully so, but if the kids trust you and you trust the kids, they don't run home and say, "We talked about *this* in class today." Or even if they do, I'm cool with that. I'm going to say, "Well, this is the context, and this is what I said about it."

Accountability versus Freedom

Sarah also talked about the difficulty of balancing external demands with her desire to have a high-functioning culture: "I feel sometimes it's difficult to stay true to what I believe, or what I've read, or what students have taught me is best for them in this high-stakes, high-accountability, results-driven world."

While Sarah feels the need to respond to such external pressures, she has learned to define them as another piece of data that helps her decide what she will do. She empowers herself to do this by continuously focusing on her highest purpose: the development of her students. While many teachers may feel constrained or even shackled by changing external pressures, when Sarah closes the door of her classroom, she chooses to be in the moment and to be creative. Sarah is self-empowering, but this does not mean that she ignores demands from the external world. She recognizes the importance of many of these external pressures but still tries to act consistently with her internal values.

Sarah often finds the current rhetoric about teacher accountability maddening, but she also says, "I'm not saying that I don't fall victim to that because I totally will get worked up and upset. But when I look at reality, I have a lot of freedom. A lot of it's on me." After claiming she is responsible for her level of freedom, Sarah made a surprising statement: "But the kids give you that; I don't think that comes from anywhere else."

We asked her to clarify this statement. She first talked about the profound conversations and the deep learning that takes place in her classroom. She then indicated that her students give her the freedom to hold such conversations:

> When you really think about it, they [students] are running the show. They kind of decide *This is what we're doing today*. I don't mean they totally decide, but you know they have quite a bit of power and if they don't like you—they're teenagers, they're resourceful—they will figure out how to get the principal in your classroom all the time, how to have their parents call all the time and hassle you. So I feel like the kids are the ones who allow you to do the work that you want to do.

In life many of us make assumptions that limit our effectiveness. If we take only the directive perspective and define teaching in terms of formal, hierarchical authority, it follows that those who are below us have an obligation to comply. But when we do this, we forget that people also have free will. If students are dissatisfied with how a teacher treats them, they may use their creativity to sabotage the learning process. Sarah is expressing a more complex view. She assumes the responsibility of the directive perspective but also recognizes that what she is trying to achieve is a process that is co-created with her students.

Sarah: I bring my whole self into the classroom, and I ask my kids to bring their whole selves into the classroom. If I do anything right, it is that. I feel lucky because I found this job where I get to be myself—emotional and funny and goofy and silly and excited with them.

Engaging the Red and Green Quadrants

Early in her career, Sarah feared the loss of control. She worried that "the wheels would come off and my classroom would explode." But she eventually learned that she could relax control and trust her students to engage at a high level. In doing this she has learned how to connect attributes of the red and green quadrants. Planning and procedures (red quadrant) underlie her ability to foster a creative and adaptive learning environment (green quadrant).

> I think that has something to do with human nature. We're so consumed with holding on to control. We assume that when we let go, something bad will happen. In my classroom only good things have come of letting go. I mean, I plan my butt off, and I structure everything...but in that 50 minutes that I have with them [students], I really try to let go of the results...[of] where I thought we were going to be at the end of the 50 minutes and know that if I design materials and introduce ideas that matter to them, it's going to work. They will make it work.

For people who put great emphasis on gaining and maintaining control, as Sarah initially did, the notion of surrendering it may seem illogical. But the fear of surrendering control may prevent a teacher from accessing the benefits of the green quadrant. To nurture a high-functioning culture, Sarah has learned to integrate her practice across the quadrants (see figure 4.1). In the next section, we try to understand Sarah's unusual claim: "They will make it work."

Figure 4.1 *Culture-Building as a Powerful Practice*

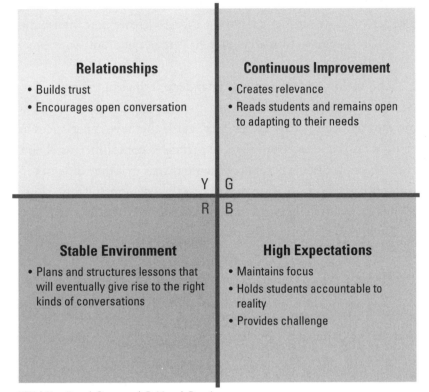

KEY | Y: yellow | G: green | B: blue | R: red

Collective Learning

When Sarah focuses on learning and pays attention to what her students are teaching her, something important often happens: "When the energy is high…I can look out and see it;…it's literally something. I don't know how to describe it. I can feel there is energy in the room. Everyone's brainwaves are making connections or making motion or something like that."

Sarah is talking about what Diana called the emergence of the "living beast" or what Aaron called the "different realm." It is the time when collective learning peaks and students tend to produce their best results.

Sarah marvels at the collaborative products that emerge. The examples range from creating satiric commercials to executing a Mother's Day brunch. To Sarah these kinds of activities are about more than the related content standards and the specific artifacts that students create. Through these activities students encounter or even co-create new information. As they do they have to marry the new (green quadrant) with the old (red quadrant).

This integrative process may alter deep frames of reference. Sarah says that this process challenges what students previously valued and how they previously saw themselves. With the new experiences and perspectives that arise from these experiences comes increased confidence. Students discover that they can do things that they did not think they were capable of doing. In the process they demonstrate their ability to "encounter anything, any kind of situation and be able...to figure it out." Sarah also claims that the process fosters a love of learning. She is suggesting that the co-creative perspective adds great value to the directive perspective.

In this book we meet teachers who create cultures of collective learning. These dynamics sometimes give rise to a shared mind. A *shared mind* emerges when individuals contribute to the group's understanding of a topic, but those same individuals do not "own" their contributions. Because the contributions arose out of the dialogue, they belong to the group.[2] These experiences can transform students' conceptions of who they are and what they can accomplish. Students become like the empowered person who teaches them—lifelong learners. This perspective on teaching and learning goes beyond the assumptions of the directive perspective. To conclude this chapter, we discuss three aspects of co-creative practice that make this kind of collective learning possible: the facilitative role, the stance toward error, and the view of group membership (see figure 4.2).

Role: Instructor versus Facilitator

One of the keys to collective learning is the role of facilitator. As we saw in chapter 1, some people equate the role of teacher with the role of *instructor*—a person with expertise who disseminates information to students. Many of the HETs we interviewed view their teaching as going

Figure 4.2 *Enabling Collective Learning*

	Directive Perspective	**Co-creative Perspective**
Role	Instructor	Facilitator
Stance toward error	Avoid error	Learn from error
Group membership	Expect outliers	Expect full participation

beyond the directive perspective. They also take on the role of *facilitator*— a person who acts as a catalyst of the collective learning process.

The goal of facilitation is to build a culture of inquiry, to include everyone in the discussions, and to help students speak openly about key issues, including their experiences with failure. The process is co-created by the facilitator and the students in the classroom. The facilitator improvises in real time, and when the process peaks, the students engage in the conceptually elusive process of self-organization.

In the directive perspective, students are seen as individual actors. Through the process of facilitation, students and their teacher become interconnected and interdependent. Learning becomes a collaborative process, and cohesion is important.

Teachers who facilitate tend to focus on the ways that students speak to one another and encourage them to use positive language. There is an emphasis on such character traits as tolerance, kindness, and forgiveness. They are sensitive to their students and craft the discussions in ways that develop students' trust and inspire students' confidence in the teacher's ability to bring them closer together. Trust stems from the knowledge that "I'm not going to embarrass them." Trust is a core aspect of psychological safety.

Collaborative learning is a challenge. It often begins with teaching students what it means to learn as a group. As one HET explained, "I kind of approach teaching just like I'm coaching....Our classroom is run like a team, and when one member of that team is not necessarily doing what they need to do, it does start to bring down the other members of the team. What can we do as a group, as a community, to bring that person back up and to make them feel better about themselves and to feel like they're offering something to the conversation?"

This quote alludes to a key aspect of collective learning: when even one student deviates, it can destroy the collective learning process. In highly effective groups, there is often a transformation from negative peer pressure to positive peer pressure. Once this transformation occurs, there is less need for the teacher to "police" the class. The students keep one another in line. In this quote the teacher adds an additional expectation: not only should the student be brought back in but the group should help the student feel good about him- or herself. The group should help the student feel like a valued contributor to the conversation. This statement suggests a deep sensitivity to how groups function and a high expectation for how students should behave. This kind of sensitivity can be seen in the following sections as well.

Stance toward Error: Avoid Error versus Learn from Error

In the process of collective learning, many HETs talk about error as an essential aspect of their classroom. The collective learning process is a journey. One teacher told us, "I don't know if the students can always know the flow of where we're going because sometimes it's formulating as we're going....We have a goal or objective in mind, so in that sense we have an idea of where we're going;…we're just not sure how we're going to get there.

Under the assumptions of hierarchy (red quadrant), the teacher knows exactly where the group is going and provides the path to get there. Under the assumptions of emergence (green quadrant), the group is going to a place of excellence in learning. Excellence is, by definition, a departure from the norm.

In each episode of collective learning, the group is going somewhere it has never been before. Hence it is impossible to "know" exactly how the group will get there. The teacher has a plan, but in the emergent learning process the plan is often left behind. Emergent learning is often characterized by false starts and dead ends. These "errors" are important because they teach us what does *not* work. Knowing what does not work is a step toward discovering how to succeed. In hierarchies people tend to hide and devalue their errors. In an emergent learning system, people have to learn how to openly acknowledge and share their errors. For this to happen, trust is essential. Effective facilitators understand this process and create environments of trust so that error can be shared.

In the amplified learning process, people learn as a collective. For example, one HET told us, "I encourage [students] to take chances. There is no penalty for wrong answers. We celebrate the chances that are taken, whether right or wrong, by congratulating them on a job well done. When things are going well, students' hands are up and they are eager to share their answers."

Some HETs use themselves as models with respect to this stance toward error. This means they are often willing to model vulnerability. Sarah told us that she sees a direct link between her own vulnerability and the willingness of her students to take the risks. She has to overcome their "resistance to participating in their own education" to facilitate the emergence of a learning community. If she wants them to express their authentic voice, she has to express her authentic voice: "You can get kids to take risks if you can create that community, [but] you have to do it first."

✒ *TEACHER'S TIP*

Sarah: If you are asking your kids to write, *you* have to write. If you don't write, you are going to get a bunch of things like "It was the day I ran away. It was bad." But if you want expressive writing—if you want them to write about feelings and emotions and the concrete details that match those emotions—you have to do it first.

Some teachers are comfortable sharing failures and calling attention to their own mistakes. Some HETs believe that when students see a teacher make a mistake and work to fix it, the students become more likely to take responsibility for fixing their own mistakes. Sarah told us that, in her first year of teaching, she "made a million mistakes." Yet she also says that she was learning in real time. She was fully present with her students. This suggests that both she and her students were engaged in a system of mutual learning in which error was an important source of knowledge.

Group Membership: Expect Outliers versus Full Participation

From a directive perspective, it is normal to expect that some students on some days will be disengaged. The question is *What does a teacher do about these outliers?*

The tendency can be either to focus all of your attention on those who are disengaged, thereby guaranteeing that little learning is happening, or to pay attention only to those who readily join in. An alternative approach is to engage both "the willing" and "the outliers." It is important to reach both groups because the absence of either tends to block collective learning. As one HET told us, "If one person fails, we all fail." Some teachers start with those who are easy and then convert those who are not. One HET told us:

> I hear about these children who are hard-to-reach kids at the beginning of the year, and in my mind I devise a plan for how I'm going to reach out to these kids, to include them, and to get them involved in my class. Most kids come into the room fully knowing what a teacher is and what [my] role is as a teacher, and they're easy. It's these outsiders—they're on the boundaries—that you have to work on to bring into the fold....[When the outliers buy in,] there's such a chemistry going on in the classroom of everybody collaborating and participating....Everything runs smoothly, and the process of learning and teaching becomes enjoyable and easy....It is exhausting emotionally to have boys and girls in the classroom who are not learning enough.

Some HETs think about outliers during class, and they continue to think about them after class is over. They spend time reflecting on who is not participating and why. They invest time in thinking about how to achieve full participation. This may include systematic reflection at the end of the workday. For example, one HET described her experience with a particular student:

I think about this little girl that I had last year....I had to make a serious point to clue in on her every day because she would avoid it....She just didn't like to talk...and I didn't want to push it. You know with that kind of child, you have to be very sensitive, so I started making a record of everything we talked about...[and] what time of day was the best to talk to her....I told her, "You know what? You can come see me any day after school is out, and we can talk about this or I can help you with your math." She came every day....She just needed to have a connection outside of all the chaos.

Another HET talked about a project she took on to reengage a group of four students who had dissociated themselves from their teachers and classmates. She could not wait until they entered eighth grade, when she would have them in her math class: "They were four young, withdrawn, bitter, staring boys. They never spoke to their seventh-grade teachers... and used their eyes to defy any act of kindness....They stared at the other children. They stared at the teachers. They just refused to be a part of anything."

She knew she had to be patient to engage these students, so she started out very carefully with "an occasional compliment" about the skulls on their clothing. "Compliments gave way to questions about the lovely skull jewelry," which the boys wouldn't answer. After a few weeks, she began to roll her chair over to sit with them during class:

They weren't speaking yet, but their eyes followed me to see if I would be joining them. The day I exclaimed, "Oh, that is the prettiest red skull! Can I touch it?" was the turning point. They erupted with grins and surprisingly sweet, boyish giggles. We never looked back. They visit my class from time to time. They give me discounted pizza at Pizza Hut when they are on shift, and they are *all* working their way through college. Each of them is pursuing a career in the medical field. These boys represent so many low-self-esteem, special education, beaten-down-by-life students who have crossed my path. A little effort, a little love, a little attention, and a few smiles can make such a big difference.

Then she noted, "Once I accepted them, the rest of their class accepted them....It was just wonderful to watch them become part of the world again. I don't know what they could have spiraled into, but they came back to us." The boys began to connect with the class, the teacher, and their own learning.

Summary

In this chapter we learned about practice that grows out of the yellow quadrant through Sarah's journey from teacher-centered practice as a beginning teacher, to student-centered practice, and finally to learning-centered practice. We note that the process of collective learning is at the heart of the co-creative perspective. We suggest that three shifts may play a role in the transition to collective learning. The first is a shift from seeing teaching as instruction to seeing it as both instruction and facilitation. The second is a shift from avoiding error to learning from error. The third is a shift from expecting outliers to expecting full engagement of all students. As Jung suggests in the epigraph, Sarah recognizes that "warmth is the vital element for the growing plant and for the soul of the child."

🌰 *PLANTING SEEDS*

1. Sarah talks about the problems she experienced as a beginning teacher. Her principal advised her to begin to really pay attention and listen to her students. What have you learned about yourself as a teacher when you have had the opportunity to pay attention and really listen to your students? What changed in your practice when you did this?

2. Sarah uses the challenges she faced as a child to empathize with her students, especially those who find it difficult to engage in school. How have you used your own experiences growing up to build stronger connections with your students?

3. Many teachers struggle to integrate the yellow and blue dimensions of practice, especially in an era of increased teacher accountability. In the minds of some, accountability has taken the "fun" out of teaching. In what ways have you been able to build on your relationships with students to increase their performance?

4. Sarah relates the story of what happened in her classroom following the suicide of a student at her school. What experiences have you had with your students following a traumatic incident? How have these experiences shaped your teaching?

GROWING YOUR PRACTICE

1. Consider one child in your classroom with whom you feel you have a weak relationship. What is one practice outlined in or sparked by reading this chapter that you could use to try to reach that child this week?

2. All the teachers in this book have talked about times in which collective learning has emerged for them. Think back on your best lessons, when collective learning happened in your classroom. What were the key triggers? What was different about that lesson in comparison with other lessons you have taught? List two strategies that you can incorporate into future lessons to help trigger more of these experiences.

CHAPTER 5

Empowering the Soul: Developing Yourself

Educational institutions are full of divisive structures, of course,
but blaming them for our brokenness perpetuates the myth that the
outer world is more powerful than the inner. The external structures
of education would not have the power to divide us as deeply as
they do if they were not rooted in one of the most compelling features
of our inner landscape—fear....Fear is what distances us from our
colleagues, our students, our subjects, ourselves. Fear shuts down
those "experiments with truth" that allow us to weave a wider
web of connectedness—and thus shuts down our own capacity
to teach as well.

—Parker Palmer
The Courage to Teach

LAURIE IS A HIGH SCHOOL ENGLISH TEACHER WITH 18 YEARS OF experience. She began her career in a rural community and now teaches in a suburban school district. In many ways she personifies the epigraph by Palmer. She does not give away her power. She is not divided from her subject, her students, or herself. And her focus is on the relationship between teaching and learning and on weaving "a wider web of connectedness."[1]

We do not mean the last claim figuratively. In her classroom Laurie literally weaves a "web of connectedness." It is something she does on the first day of each school year.

CHAPTER OVERVIEW

Empowering the Soul

Through Laurie's story we explore what it means to become self-empowered. People feel self-empowered at work when they experience four qualities:

- Meaning
- Competence
- Autonomy
- Impact[2]

Our work with HETs suggests that learning accelerates when teachers first learn to empower themselves and then to empower their students (see chapter 6). Our interviews with Laurie and other HETs provide many illustrations of this possibility. We begin by learning about the "web of connectedness" she weaves each year.

Weaving a Web of Connectedness

On the first day, Laurie seats her students in a circle, holds up a ball of string, and introduces herself. While holding the end of the string, Laurie throws the ball to a student. That student introduces herself and then expresses how she wants others to see her in that community by sharing a strength, interest, or memory. Each student repeats the process, takes hold of a section of the string, and then tosses the ball to someone else. By the end of the activity, everyone is literally connected in a large web of string. Laurie then talks to her students about how the web is a metaphor for their classroom:

> When Sally is pulling on the string over here, what does that do? Well, that affects Bobby. Well, give me an example of how that translates in the classroom. Ah, you're in a group, and you didn't do your homework. Crap, Sally has to do all the work because Bobby didn't do the work, and now we've got a broken string. So how do we fix

it? Well, we've all got a piece of the string. You hand Sally back her string, and you make it work. You fix it.

Based on the activity, Laurie makes a seemingly paradoxical connection: "If we work independently but together, we can get it done better, faster, and stronger. We are all held together, and we have this safety net now in the classroom."

In encouraging students to "work independently but together," Laurie is thinking across the quadrants. She believes the work will be of a higher quality and learning will unfold at an accelerated rate as a result of this integration. This kind of community building is an example of a powerful practice. Laurie believes it produces positive outcomes that last throughout the school year: "I really believe that by having this as my primary focus, everything else in my room falls into place. Because I carefully construct our environment, I do not have issues with behavior and rules being followed. Kids feel a responsibility to me, each other, and our work."

In figure 5.1 we draw from Laurie's story to elaborate on how she has built the web activity into a powerful practice that feeds back into her classroom throughout the school year. The value of the web activity lies in the ways Laurie weaves this practice through all four quadrants of the Connect Framework and in how she continues to build on this activity throughout the school year.

School Culture

For Laurie the web activity is far more than an interesting opening exercise. It is a living metaphor for who she is, what she will create, and what students will experience. Not only does she use it to set the tone and to learn about her students, but it also serves as the core template for how she wants her classroom to operate. She builds on it daily, and, as we will see later, it creates connections with and among her students that persist after they leave her classroom at the end of the year.

At times she tries to help administrators and colleagues understand the power of community building, but this is foreign territory for some

Figure 5.1 *The Web as a Powerful Practice*

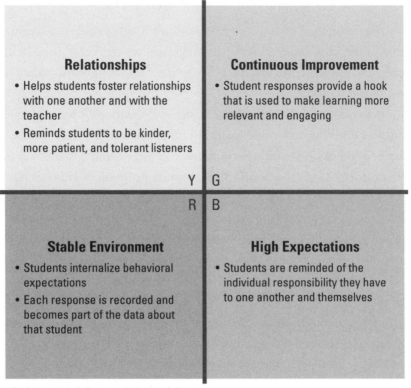

KEY | Y: yellow | G: green | B: blue | R: red

people. Perhaps because of their fears or because they are less comfortable opening themselves up as Laurie does, some denigrate Laurie's way of connecting with her students. With some pain she tells stories of administrators and colleagues who have made deriding comments about her efforts.

Just as negative peer pressure can operate among students and stifle learning, it can also operate among the adults in a school and stifle their professional growth. The liberation of excellence usually involves transcending conventional assumptions. When this happens fears may arise, leading others to react with derision. This is true not only in schools but in all organizations. People who feel disempowered are unlikely to become positive outliers. But how does someone become self-empowering?

Self-Empowerment

Laurie tells of an interesting transition in her life. She described how earlier in her career she found it difficult to let go at the end of the school year when students moved to the next grade: "I [was] getting fed from the kids externally. Despite the strength of my core beliefs, I needed that external adulation and that connection and community."

When Laurie had a child of her own, her hunger for approval from her students declined, and she had an insight: "I realized that I've got everything I need. It's *not* an external thing."

Laurie's perspective began to change. She gained increased confidence that she was doing a good job. Her motivation became more intrinsic: "I see the lights in their eyes and that's enough. It's not the positive phone calls from parents or the recommendation from the principal to be on some committee or something. I'm done proving myself."

As she continued to develop, Laurie became a more autonomous, internally directed person: "I don't have to go to the principal and say, 'Hey, I just wanted to let you know I'm involved in this and I'm doing this.' I know principals want to know that stuff so that they can keep tabs on their employees, but I don't go to them anymore."

Laurie also indicated that she no longer measures herself through the eyes of others. While she continually assesses how she is doing, her reference is not the performance of others. She notes that being more internally directed allows her to listen, open up, and learn: "I like hearing what other people have done in their teaching, and I let it sit and simmer longer. Then I try to see what I can take from them to make me better, but it's not a competitive thing anymore....When I was younger, I think I wanted to know that I was on par with everybody else."

Laurie has learned how to empower herself. Her environment did not change. Her principal did not change the nature of their relationship. Instead Laurie changed how she perceived herself and her work. In the sections that follow, we consider the four shifts that are associated with being self-empowered. These shifts are summarized in figure 5.2.

Figure 5.2 *Shifts to Self-Empowerment*

	Directive Perspective	Co-creative Perspective
Meaning	Job	Calling
Competence	Professional confidence	Adaptive confidence
Autonomy	Constrained	Authentic
Impact	Comprehension	Lifelong learners

 RESEARCH FOUNDATIONS

Empowerment

Research by Gretchen Spreitzer[3] suggests that people experience self-empowerment when they:

- Feel *meaning* and purpose in their work
- Feel a sense of *competence*—that they can do their job well[4]
- Have a sense of *autonomy*—that they have self-determination in how they do their work
- Feel a sense of *impact*—that their work is indeed making a difference

Together these four dimensions reflect an active, rather than passive, orientation to a person's job. In other words the experience of empowerment depends on all four dimensions; if any single dimension is missing, the experience of empowerment will be limited.[5] For example, if people have discretion to make decisions (i.e., self-determination) but the decisions they make are unimportant (i.e., they lack a sense of meaning), they will not feel empowered. Alternatively, if people believe they can make an impact but do not feel like they have the skills and the abilities to do their job well (i.e., they lack a sense of competence), they will not feel empowered. Thus employees feel psychologically empowered when they experience all four dimensions.

Research in education suggests that some teachers are self-empowered despite being embedded in an environment that may not be particularly empowering—where "teachers' work roles are routine and repetitive, where teachers are isolated from peers, and where the pressures of time and understaffing leave minimal time for doing anything new or different."[6] This is important because it suggests that teachers need not wait to be empowered by their principals or the system as a whole.

Why care about empowerment? We know that empowered individuals are more satisfied with and committed to their work.[7] They are more effective and innovative, and they have the courage to take initiative to try new things.[8] Empowered people care more about their work and sustain their energy at work for longer periods of time. In short, empowered people are more likely to be transformative to themselves and others.[9]

The Meaning Dimension of Self-Empowerment

Many people work to make a living. They have a job. Laurie feels that teaching is not only her job but also her calling or personal passion. She lives out her calling by developing deep connections with her students and encouraging her students to make deep connections with one another. Her objective is to teach them to live life meaningfully. She makes a claim much like a claim made by Sarah earlier in the book: "I love teaching English because it gives me a vehicle to teach [students] how to be better people. If there was a course in just being nice and being a good person, and knowing how to talk to people, how to make them feel good about what you're doing, how to make yourself feel good about what you're doing, I'd teach it. I would love it, but they don't offer that in high school. They offer English."

This is a claim that ties back to the epigraph by Palmer. Laurie wants her students to overcome their fears and more fully embrace others and themselves. She wants to build an empowering community because it will give students the courage and the support they need to empower themselves. It may be that they create a mutually reinforcing system where learning accelerates and lives are changed.

The web activity is one of the many ways that Laurie crafts her work to fulfill her calling.[10] At the end of the activity, Laurie cuts up the web created with the string. The next day she hands each student a piece of that string. During the year she gives bonus points on the midterm and semester exams to students who still have the string. The string becomes symbolic of the deep connection students develop with her and with one another.

When Laurie taught eighth grade, she collected the pieces of string at the end of the year and used them to tie together two small feathers and a twig. She then gave one to each of her students along with the quote *There are two things we should give our children: one is roots; the other is wings.*

For the eighth-grade graduation ceremony, her students would pin the twig-and-feathers to their clothes or tie it around their wrists. Now that she teaches high school, she gives the same gift to her seniors. When she goes to graduation parties, students often have their piece of the web on their graduation table right next to their scrapbook from kindergarten. The students seem to believe that the experience of having been part of the web is a memory worth celebrating.

The string is also a reminder that the web is not broken at the end of the school year. Although Laurie and her students all move on to do different things, they are still connected by their shared experiences. At the high school where Laurie teaches, seniors can select a teacher to hand them their diploma. This past year 14 seniors asked Laurie to present them their diploma. She had the opportunity to teach many of these seniors twice: once as eighth-graders and again after she moved to the high school. She wrote each of the 14 students a letter in which she expressed her enduring belief in the power of community and connection:

> The letter to the 14 kids was based on the metaphor of 18 years, that they are 18 years old and I am 18 years in the profession…and how

we've ended up at this point together and how we've helped each other over the past five years to develop who we are, where we are, what our community is, what we believe in, how we communicate, how we rely on each other, and how that reciprocity is invaluable and it establishes our community....We can draw back on those experiences of those five years and know that we are better, stronger, faster, smarter for having each other and each other's influence.

While Laurie gladly accepts her paycheck, it is not money that causes her to write letters like this one. It is her sense of calling. Teaching is who she is. She loves what she does.

✦ TEACHER'S TIP

Laurie: No one can afford to slip into malaise or apathy about the work of teaching. Leave time for reflection and self-assessment. Never fear tweaking or completely overhauling a lesson, even to the point of saying to the kids, "Yesterday was bad, wasn't it? I could see I wasn't getting through to you/that assignment was too ambiguous/the discussion fell flat....I prepared a do-over for today—are you with me? Let's try this out." Openly showing humility, fallibility, and accountability are life lessons that students will never forget. Keeping things real is a testament to your character and a way to stay fresh when things seem most trying. If you are in the right profession, teaching shouldn't feel like work.

Calling

In our interviews and workshops with HETs, there were many illustrations of the notion of calling. Some speak of teaching as their "destiny," "identity," or "life calling." They love working with children, and they want to make a lasting difference. One HET told us, "Sometimes [students] come in with negative history, bogged down from the world, and with negative opinions of themselves....I feel like it's part of my job to transform their thinking, and you can transform their lives [by transforming] how they see themselves. It's not just about the content area. It's about how they see themselves in the world."

People who find meaning in their work tend to be fully engaged.[11] We often heard the word *passion* in our interviews with HETs. At the end of each of our HET workshops, we asked what most impressed the teachers about spending a day with other HETs. A constant theme was passion. One teacher, for example, summed up her observations of the other HETs in the room: "I would say that is the number one criterion: You have to care. You have to care a lot. You do not just care about success. You teach to have successful students and not just for this year. You teach to impact their lives."

Interestingly, passion can have different starting points. For some it starts with the subject matter and spills over to the students: "I have a passion for history. I want my kids to feel that passion. My passion for teaching them is really rooted in the fact that I love what I am teaching."

For others it starts with the children, and the subject matter is less an issue: "I don't think it's necessarily a passion for teaching because I'm not passionate about parent/teacher conferences or in-services. It's a passion for kids because when they walk in my door, those are my kids. I'm going to fight for you, I'm going to protect you, I'm going to fuss on you, but you are *my* kids."

Not every HET is drawn to teaching by passion; some have to first figure out what drives them. For example, one HET recounted having second thoughts about becoming a teacher because he did not enjoy his student-teaching experience. After graduating he subbed for a year and a half in all kinds of schools and at many grade levels: "That's where I learned where I wanted to be, what kind of kids I wanted to work with. I found out that I had a calling and a drive for lower-income kids where they might not be getting that love. I feel like God placed me there. I had to wander a long time in the wilderness—it seemed like, anyway—before I wound up where I am....This is year number 10 for me, and I love it."

Like all teachers, HETs go through rough patches in their careers. Many also mentioned aspects of the job that they dislike, such as waking up early, grading papers, doing bureaucratic paperwork, and attending meetings that have little to do with teaching kids. But as one HET describes, the joy of pursuing a passion can outweigh the perceived downsides:

I've had opportunities to try some other things, but I keep going back to really the area that I like most about education: working with the students in the classroom. I've tried teaching teachers and being on leadership teams and curriculum, things like that, but still I want to go back to the classroom. That's where I enjoy spending my time. It is work, a lot of work, tiring, but it's fulfilling. I look forward to my summers off, so to speak, to kind of rejuvenate, and I kind of reflect on what I've done, but then I look forward to going back the next year once again, having a new group of students, and just being in the classroom with them, teaching.

Some teachers may see teaching as a calling. They not only earn a living but also find deep satisfaction in what they do.

The Competence Dimension of Self-Empowerment

Competence is about being good at what you do. It often is reflected in a person's self-confidence. Confidence means being self-assured. It is the knowledge that you can rely on yourself as you engage in a certain activity. When an activity has some degree of repetition and a person has previously excelled in the activity, he or she tends to have confidence.

Adaptive Confidence

Adaptive confidence is more complex than confidence. *Adaptive* means being able to learn, adjust, or change. *Adaptive confidence* is the willingness to engage in new challenges with the belief that you will be able to learn and adapt in real time. Some people are slow to engage in a new activity because it is outside their comfort zone. Their fears keep them from engaging in what might be a useful experience. Adaptive confidence can include learning your way through challenges and mistakes. Empowered people are less fearful and more confident, and they take accountability for things that others do not.[12]

Laurie provides an example of learning from a mistake. This experience transformed her perspective of her role as a teacher and helped her develop a deeper sense of accountability to her students.

Early in her career, Laurie had a challenging group of boys. She knew they were regularly cheating and planned to catch them. She intentionally left out an answer sheet to a different test than the one they were taking. They copied it. She then marched them down to the principal's office. The boys were disciplined and were subsequently sent back to the class-room. The principal then closed the door and told Laurie to sit down. He asked her questions and helped her take a deeper look into what had transpired. Eventually, he told her, "You can't do that to people. They are not just kids; they are people."

Laurie protested that they had been cheating, and she knew this was a way to prove it. The principal replied, "It is dishonest. You can't do that." While she was at first offended, gradually Laurie realized that her own dishonesty was as blatant as what she was condemning. The discovery of her own hypocrisy, which Laurie recounted to us with tears, had a great impact on her. What did she learn? She explained: "I still feel horrible about it. I can still see the kids' faces, and I get all teary-eyed, but that was a huge lesson for me because those kids matter, too. The reason a kid cheats is because they feel like they can't survive. And if a kid can't survive in my classroom, what kind of environment am I creating? That was a huge lesson."

The conventional assumption is that cheating is a failure of the student, not the teacher. Yet empowered people tend to be slower to point the finger of blame. Instead they are more likely to examine their own contribution to the situation. Before they act to correct others' behavior, they put themselves in the place of the others. Ultimately, the intent to change something in others requires that they first seek to change them-selves. This kind of adaptive confidence often leads to new and often counterintuitive paths of action.

The ability to see your own hypocrisy and then change yourself is a very powerful form of learning. It not only involves gaining new knowledge but also results in feeling better about yourself. Having such experiences may give rise to adaptive confidence.

Laurie also gave an example of trying a new strategy early in her teaching career that backfired. In an effort to reinforce the value of making mistakes, she painted a picture of herself as fallible and imperfect. Her students misinterpreted her disclosures as a sign of incompetence, and she began to lose the class. Her response is an illustration of personal accountability and adaptive confidence: "I said, 'Hey, do you guys think I can do this? Have I built up enough trust?' We pulled out the web—the string thing again—and I said, 'Can you sit down on the floor and go through this again?…Where have I let you down so far?' We talked about it, and thank goodness I only had three 90-minute periods. I came home and cried that whole night. I just went, 'All right, we've got to pull this back in,' but it was hard."

In the account Laurie took a risk. In the midst of that failure, she joined with her students and invited authentic feedback. The feedback hurt. She grieved the failure but reconnected with her students to get back on track. Her purpose was more important than her ego.

Seeking Out Feedback to Build Competence

Laurie continually invites her students and their parents to give her authentic feedback. One of her favorite nights of the year is meet-the-teacher night. Because of the success Laurie has had with prior students, parents often expect that their children will be successful just because Laurie is their teacher. She uses this meeting as an opportunity to set the record straight. Here again we see the presentation of an authentic and vulnerable self:

> Just because you're here doesn't mean that I'm going to be this panacea for your kid. They still have to do the work. And I might not be able to address them where they are right away. It might take me until November. So I have to let the parents know that I don't have all the answers, and I don't know everything. And all these years of experience, and all the books I've read, and all the conferences I've attended help me to be who I am. But that still doesn't mean that I'm going to be who I need to be for your kid, and I understand the value in that—that just because you're sitting in here doesn't guarantee anything. I'm still going to be fallible, and you still need to give me feedback about what your kid is or is not getting in the classroom because I might not be addressing who they are, where they are, and what they need….I don't ever want to lose sight of that kind of core value.

In Laurie's statement there is an assumption about growth, but "that still doesn't mean that I'm going to be who I need to be for your kid."

Despite her years of experience, she meets new and unique challenges. To reach every student, she has to act, take feedback, experiment, and learn. She is always seeking feedback so that she can embrace the reality of the present moment while pursuing the realization of the potential in the next moment. This orientation to real-time learning suggests that she is becoming the best teacher in her again and again.

TEACHER'S TIP

> **Laurie:** Prior to meet-the-teacher night, I have the parents write a letter about their students—telling me about them— their dreams, their favorite memories, and, of course, their strengths and weaknesses in both school in general and English specifically. This way, as the year is beginning, I know something about all of my families and their expectations for their kids. It helps me to put faces and names to their stories. Almost all the parents close the letters with "Thank you for wanting to know about my child." It helps them see that I am interested in teaching kids, not just English.

Real-time learning means paying attention to both verbal and nonverbal signals. One of our interviewees told us:

> I am at my best when I can pick up the signals from my students that allow me to adjust plans to meet the situation. I have been able to get better and better at this over the years, which has helped me to be at my best for the students more of the time. These signals may involve problems a student is having or whether the students are grasping the material being taught. By reading these signals and adjusting accordingly, I can do a better job getting through and helping students be better learners.

Many HETs shared that they are constantly looking and listening for evidence of student learning. When an activity does not result in the desired learning, they tend to reflect on the problem as their own failure, not as the failure of the students. They then tend to move forward by experimenting. They are often willing to "step out of the box and take risks to increase student learning."

Realizing Uniqueness

When challenges arise that seem threatening, the natural reaction may be to suppress them. Teachers with adaptive confidence are more likely to engage challenges and learn. Teachers who keep learning and improving are continually creating better versions of themselves. And the emerging selves are likely to be even more unique and more creative. Just as a great musician is likely to have a unique musical voice, an HET is likely to have a unique orientation to practice: "If you're always trying to [copy] what everybody else is doing, then you're not going to find your own way. When you have a chance to find your own way, that's when you're going to be the best teacher you're going to be. If you take a minute to step out of that box, then you can find yourself."

The last sentence suggests that great teaching is about finding yourself, about being the best teacher in you again and again. That teacher is unique, even different from the one who exists in you today. This process of finding our best, unique self may involve transcending our own fears, as suggested by Palmer in the epigraph. Another HET described this process: "It is about letting go of the fear—of administrators, of the state, and of the test scores. You are not a test score. No one is. You don't have to go by the textbook."

When people make this change, they may become more internally directed. They may become more likely to draw on their own strengths. They may tap into aspects of their life that they are passionate about and use them to teach with an increasing sense of passion: "I think that is a key. Not everybody can do a cartwheel. Not everybody can play guitar, but there's something you're already good at and passionate about that you can relate to what you're doing."

It seems that HETs trust themselves to learn in real time. They believe in pushing forward until they figure it out. In fact, the phrase *figure it out* was frequently used. HETs seem to have great faith in the power of learning in real time. Robert Quinn, in one of his earlier books, calls this "building the bridge as you walk on it."[13] It is often a process of transformative learning, and it empowers the person who engages in it, leaving them with the capacity to empower others.

The Autonomy Dimension of Self-Empowerment

Laurie believes that a key to building the web of connectedness is how people talk. She speaks a lot about helping students "find themselves so that they know what they're saying, why they're saying it, to whom they're saying it [and] for what purposes."

She believes that one of her central roles as a teacher is to speak authentically with students so that they can learn to empower themselves. She wants students to feel comfortable taking initiative and doing things their own way. The implication is that authenticity and autonomy are linked.

Laurie told us about one of her students who got into serious trouble and was going to court. He was worried about how others might judge him because of his ethnicity. She shared the advice she gave him prior to his court date: "How are you going to present yourself to the judge? What have you learned this year about your voice? Which words are you going to choose? How are you going to say them and with what cadence? When you go to court, you give them what you know and you ask for forgiveness because you're 15....You need to have some punishment for it, but you've got to make sure you present yourself in the truest sense, the sense that I see in the classroom."

This statement has many implications. The fact that Laurie expects a 15-year-old to enter an intimidating situation with a proactive stance suggests that she understands and teaches empowerment. The fact that she wants him to take accountability (blue quadrant) while also revealing himself in the "truest sense" (yellow quadrant) suggests that she teaches her students to engage in powerful practices. It also suggests that he will be most powerful or autonomous when he is most authentic. The fact that the boy reveals his truest self in the class suggests that her classroom is a community of authentic conversation and a place where students become engaged at the deepest level. The fact that she can speak to the boy with such frankness suggests that they have an authentic and trusting relationship.

While Laurie is capable of frankness, she realizes that she also needs to adapt her voice so that others can hear and accept it. She pointed out that she was talking to us in a way that is very different from how she speaks to her nine-year-old son. She adapts her voice to each situation. This ability to adapt gives her great range. She can work effectively with the highest and lowest academic levels because "I meet them where they are on their own terms; I say things differently to them."

While her choice of words, cadence, and tone change based on her audience, she notes that her message is consistent and unwavering. This is possible because she reads situations and talks to "different people in the way they need to hear it" (green quadrant) while she stays connected to her "core values" (red quadrant). She can use different words and give the same message because she knows who she is.

TEACHER'S TIP

Laurie: For two years now, I have taught several periods of two different classes: Honors English 10, where some kids are reading at a college level, and an intervention reading class, where the average reading level is fifth grade. I am grateful to have these distinct, homogeneous groups, for I can use the vocabulary, sentences, anecdotes, and materials best suited to each class. Even within each class, my register shifts to accommodate individual students—I have to know how to deliver my core message on *their* terms. The girl who loves softball will understand home runs; the kid whose father is a professor will understand advanced degrees; the kids who live in the trailer park will understand hard work—all will get the message about making progress.

Self-Determination despite a Disempowering System

While many HETs operate in school settings that they see as supportive, some feel that their context provides only limited support. Some feel isolated; some even feel that school cultures punish excellence. At the earliest HET workshops, some teachers shared that they had never been shown their value-added scores. Others were instructed by their administrators to keep their participation in the HET workshop a secret. Singling out teachers as excellent is sometimes seen as a break from the culture of *We're all equal here.*

While many administrators are described as going out of their way to be helpful, others are not available. HETs also speak of increasing encroachment from the state or district in terms of dictating not only what to teach but also how and when to teach it. Such programs, based on normal assumptions of top-down control, are constructed to standardize teaching. While these systems are not meant to be oppressive, HETs often feel that the system is "trying to sabotage what you have going." That is, well-meaning policy makers and administrators sometimes undermine excellence by forcing everyone into a particular mold. That structure may be useful and necessary for some, but it also gets in the way of others.

One HET shared a personal example: "When I moved to seventh grade, I thought I would be successful because of all my previous experiences, and I wasn't. I was expected to be on the same page on the same day as all the other teachers, and my whole teaching style had changed. I was forced to be a cookie cutter and not myself. This year I didn't listen. I did what I thought would be the right thing to do, and my scores went back up."

Much of this can be attributed to the orthodox culture of many schools. Some of it can also be attributed to the recent emergence of top-down accountability systems. Sometimes schools are pushed to be competitive, "like a business," and colleagues are slow to share their best ideas. The point is that, in many cases, conventional school cultures are reluctant to single out and recognize excellence. Excellence, by definition, is deviance. It may be positively deviant, but it is still deviance. An individual who enacts excellence must transcend these norms. To do this the person must be intrinsically motivated and self-empowered.

Autonomy within the System

Our interviewees tended to be focused. They spoke of the many distractions and roadblocks that crop up, but they also tended to "go around them" or, in some cases, "knock them down" because "the learning has to keep going on." For example, Diana told us, "I intentionally separate myself from political aspects of teaching. I focus on the kids and the content and the work I have at hand. I intentionally block out different evaluation systems and things like that. I have a screen, and that filters out what is going to affect my teaching and what is going to affect my students; and if it doesn't affect my students and my teaching, I don't put a lot of focus or emphasis on it."

Similarly, another HET shared, "You have to do what's best for the kids. The district might frown on some things that I do, but so be it. I think I know how kids can succeed, and I think that I have a strong sense of how I can get them to learn and love science, so I kind of just flatly do my own thing and try to keep going. I think you have to do what's right for the kids."

This intense focus is not the same as rebelliousness. Most HETs have effective working relationships with principals and other persons in authority. Aaron, for example, speaks of developing "relationships with administrators the same way you do with parents. You put your time in, do what you need to do, show up day in and day out, and you go over and above." As a result, Aaron notes, "I've had administrators…because they see the results of what some of the teachers are doing, they allow us a little bit of freedom and latitude, the ability to experiment and try some new things. They allow us a voice at the table."

HETs are empowered because they trust themselves. Because they trust themselves, they tend to have the capacity to help others obtain their desired outcomes.

Making Decisions that Push the Boundaries

The relative autonomy of HETs links back to their purpose and the meaning they derive from pursuing it. HETs often become one with their purpose and with the needs of their students. Having a calling is empowering and allows the teacher to transcend conventional expectations. One teacher told us, "Empowerment has to do with love and passion and finding that one thing in your life that you want to pursue."

Such an orientation allows an individual to engage patterns that are beyond normal expectations. Patterns of excellence often require taking the risk to violate norms. Sometimes the violations involve small risks, and sometimes they involve larger risks. Consider the following two examples.

One HET spoke of a student from a poor family whose younger sister had open heart surgery. The teacher did all she could to prepare the student. On the day of the surgery, the student called the teacher at school eight times, and the office put all the calls through to the classroom. Upon seeing her sister for the first time after the surgery, the student became uncontrollable. She called her teacher, crying, and the teacher was able to talk her through it. No one else had been able to get the girl to calm down. Afterward the parents called to say that no one had ever cared so much for their daughter. The teacher stated, the student "called me on my cell phone. I know you're not supposed to give those numbers out, but this was a different occasion. She called me several times through the weekend. I just felt like that's what it's all about to me. That's why I was there."

Another HET talked about an incident that involved a much greater risk. A boy entered her senior English class midyear. He had been to drug rehab twice. His father declared that the boy had to get things together or "he would be out." Although the boy was not a great student, the teacher managed to develop a rapport and make some progress with him. One day as she walked through a part of the building she rarely visits, she caught the boy sneaking into the school through an inner stairwell. She asked the boy why he was not in class, but he had trouble responding: "It looked like he had cotton in his mouth, and I knew that he had been using. I said, 'You and I both know this is not good. What am I going to do with you?'"

The teacher's mind began to race with all the scenarios of how she could respond and the impact her decision would have on the student and on her career: "I should take him down to the office, but if I do, he gets kicked out of his home.... There was just that internal part of me that said I could not do that.... If he goes out and has an accident and they find out I talked to him, I'll lose my job and the judge will not be kind to me."

She took a deep breath and told the boy to call his mom from his cell phone: "He handed me the phone, and I said, 'You need to come get him, and you need to come get him now. He's been using.' She said, 'I'll be right there.'"

Both the mom and the student thanked her the next day, but she thought, *Is this really going to make a difference?* As the school year progressed, the boy began doing better, and his grades in her class improved dramatically. Years later the teacher saw him again, and he told her, "Thank you, you saved my life. I want you to know that I'm about to graduate, and I'm going to be an air traffic controller." Since that day she has seen him several times and "he's doing great."

She told us, "Sometimes you need to go with the internal direction, trusting that it's the right decision. For me that day, it was the right decision. For [the boy] that day, it was the best decision. It gives me an affirmation that I am doing one of the things that I was born to do. This *is* who I am. It's not the only thing I could have done, but it is the best thing I could have done."

This story is an example of an extreme situation, one that could have resulted in major trouble for both the student and the teacher, and we are not advocating that teachers ignore policies related to drug use. Both stories are about teachers facing uncertainty and making critical decisions in real time. In both cases the teachers put themselves at risk with the decisions they made. The rules, norms, board policy, and even the law demanded one thing; their values and their relationships with particular students demanded something else. Empowered people tend to be internally directed and are more likely to make value-driven decisions. This does not mean that they are reckless. This does not even mean that they are right in their decisions. It just means that they are more likely to act in a manner that is consistent with their values, and that sometimes means taking personal risks that may not turn out well. Life is not always simple.

The Impact Dimension of Self-Empowerment

Laurie shared one of the most painful experiences of her life. She was placed on a team with a teacher who had very poor relationships with students and with other teachers. Laurie's relationship with this teacher turned into an exhausting, disheartening, and ongoing confrontation. Laurie felt "stripped down." It was so painful that she sought help from a life coach. The life coach introduced Laurie to a core principle of jujitsu:

> Instead of catching the sword when it comes at you, a jujitsu master
> will spin and stand next to the person rather than in opposition to the

person. That made so much sense to me and categorically changed
the way I approached colleagues from that point on. If I don't agree
with you, we find out why. I stand here [to the side]. If there is a
kid whom I'm combating in class, I don't try to catch their sword.
I stand here instead [to the side]. I think that was one of the biggest
eye-opening moments for me.

From this experience Laurie learned new ways to transform conflict
into cooperation, and she continues to use these skills with her students.
To illustrate, Laurie told us of her relationship with Amy, "one of the
most combative students I've ever met in my entire life." Laurie recounted
having numerous conversations with Amy about why she needed to do
her homework. She also used humor and took advantage of after-school
activities to try to create some kind of connection with Amy. When a
dramatic, external event shook Amy, she turned to Laurie for reassurance.
As their relationship deepened, Amy started doing her homework. Laurie
notes, "I had to learn her voice. I had to find out what made her tick. I
think Amy would have fought me hard....I had to find her where she was."

Many HETs shared stories about challenging or troubled students
on whom they had a positive impact. Seeing "impact" in the life of a
student often results in extra confidence. It confirms that "you are doing
something right." Reflecting on the impact they have had on their students
helps sustain them when things get difficult: "What I love is getting to
make a difference, to transform a kid's life. I am getting to transform the
world. I did the math when I went to school to become a teacher, and
I figured out how many kids I could impact. I had this astronomical
number that I came up with. I could impact a million lives across my
career. When I get bogged down, I try to keep the big picture in mind."

Success loops back to the teacher. It becomes self-reinforcing, and
"it opens you up to do more things, to be a risk taker":

I think what I most love about teaching is knowing that every day,
when I go to my job, I'm going to have the ability to have some type
of a positive impact on a child and in some cases even adults that
are around me. I love knowing that I'm going to be going into a
situation where there are little ones looking up to me and looking

at me for guidance and knowing that what I do is going to impact them and hopefully impact them in a positive way. But it just gives me a motivation to want them to be successful, knowing that I can empower them by helping them build their self-confidence and their self-esteem.

The sense of impact occurs on two levels. The first level is associated with the directive perspective in which the student comprehends the content. Teachers experience joy when they see a child begin to understand, to move from an "I'm confused" look to an "I get it" look. HETs regularly shared accounts of how they reached troubled children who seemed impossible to reach. One, for example, told of a little girl whose mother was sent to prison. The traumatized child entered the class, climbed under her desk, and began purring like a kitten. This teacher immediately reached out to the student. She said, "It was my job to reach her." She described how she worked with the student and how the student slowly became able to do her schoolwork competently.

The second level has to do with the co-creative perspective in which the student acquires confidence and a new orientation toward learning along with the content. One HET told us, "When they read *To Kill a Mockingbird,* I want them to get mad because otherwise they're just going to sit there and do nothing. One day when they're adults, they'll actually say, 'I can do something about this' or 'I can change.'"

For many HETs the ultimate goal is to transform students' basic orientations to learning. This is often reflected in the joy they express about having a child discover the power of education, to have the student internalize the excitement of learning and thus move forward, becoming a lifelong learner and someone who thinks independently. When the latter outcome occurs, HETs believe they have truly had an impact and made the world a better place.

Another teacher shared a story that illustrates this type of transformation. She was invited to teach a lesson to a class that included a young boy who had been labeled a challenged learner: "I walked up behind him and said, 'Jimmy, that picture is so bright and colorful!' He looked up at me, slowly smiled, and replied, 'How do you like that? Yesterday I couldn't color and today I can!' That is the power of teaching: removing the limitations and opening up possibilities. It is what I love most."

As we look across these examples, we get insights into how some HETs empower themselves to make an impact on their students and sometimes even the education system. In considering the process of deep change, mythologist Joseph Campbell wrote about the hero's journey.[14] He claims that in all cultures there is a basic framework of personal transformation. A person travels into a great life challenge, experiences helplessness and failure but continues on. The person faces and transcends his or her fears. In the process the person is transformed and returns from the hardship "empowered and empowering to the community."

The last phrase suggests that empowered people have an important impact on the people around them. In building her "web of connected-ness," Laurie is not entertaining her students. Her exercise is a deliberate step in the process of culture building. Laurie, as we have seen, is a self-empowered person. She works to build a context in which her students will also become empowered. In chapter 6 we focus on how HETs empower others around them.

Modeling Humility to Instill a Mindset of Continuous Learning

In closing the discussion of empowerment, we should note that while HETs often made bold statements about their strengths, we never detected hubris. We never felt that our interviewees were self-endorsing. On the contrary we felt that while they were clearly confident, they were, para-doxically, humble.

Their humility could be attributed to the norms of education. As one HET noted, "Teachers are not supposed to toot their own horns," but the pervasiveness and the explicitness of this value across HETs suggest that it is more than this.

The kind of humility that HETs display may in fact be one clear indi-cator that a teacher has moved from professional confidence to the more complex notion of adaptive confidence. Professional confidence implies that people know what they are doing. Adaptive confidence implies that people know where they want to go, but they do not fully know how they will get there. Yet they are confident that they can move forward, constantly adjusting what they are doing to fit the unique circumstances of the moment. They will thus learn their way into the future they are trying to create.

This perspective requires humility because great teachers never know for sure what the "right thing" will look like. Some HETs describe continuously learning how to make better choices in constantly evolving circumstances. It may be that as HETs develop, they are focused on their own intrinsic standard, minimizing the tendency to make social comparisons with others. It may be that their sense of self-worth is tied to their capacity to improve. They often seem hungry to learn from any source, as another teacher told us:

> I would never know that I'm in the top 5 percent [in terms of student growth]. I don't sit around and think about how I am in comparison to other teachers. But I do think about my practice, and I'm constantly trying to improve my practice. If anything makes me a great teacher, it's probably that I'm not comparing myself to everyone else, but I'm willing to take in ideas from a lot of other people and use their practices and my practices and use the kids' ideas. I have said probably the two biggest things I need as a teacher are flexibility and a lack of dignity because there are a lot of things I do that seem completely absurd outside the context of my classroom. But in the classroom, if I want kids to engage and learn, then maybe I have to get over my own dignity and this sense of how I want them to revere me. What I really want is for them to engage with me. If they're engaged with me, then they're engaged in what we're doing.

This statement indicates that the teacher is continuously trying to improve, has grown past the conventional tendency to make social comparisons, and is doing unique things that would appear unusual elsewhere. This is the statement of a person who is becoming increasingly autonomous and competent.

Summary

In this chapter we draw on the empowerment literature, which suggests that empowered people have a sense of meaning, competence, autonomy, and impact. From Laurie's story we learn how HETs, through a strong sense of meaning, may come to see their work not only as a job for which they get paid but also as a calling or source of deep meaning in their lives. We learn how, through a sense of competence, teachers may grow from a sense of professional confidence, in which they feel comfortable in situations they control, to adaptive confidence, in which they believe they can learn what to do in real time. We learn how, through a sense of autonomy, teachers may evolve from a sense of constraint to greater authenticity. And through a sense of impact, we can see how teachers may shift from seeing desired outcomes as comprehending the content to seeing desired outcomes as the transformation of identity in which students emerge as lifelong learners. Through self-empowerment it is possible to deal with what Palmer describes as the "divisive structures of education" and transcend the fear that "distances us from our colleagues, our students, our subjects and ourselves."

PLANTING SEEDS

1. Laurie uses the web activity to create an integrated learning community that allows people to take on a collective identity while maintaining an individual identity. In this connected state, there is less fear, and the participants can access new resources and can do and learn things that they cannot learn or do individually. Have you ever experienced this? What was done to make this experience possible?

2. Laurie gives each student a piece of string representing the web. Students often place their "piece of the web on their graduation table right next to their scrapbook from kindergarten." Why would the string become such a revered object? What are the implications of your answer? Do you have an exercise that authentically connects you to your students?

3. Laurie describes a shift from an external to an internal orientation: "I see the lights in their eyes and that's enough. It's not the positive phone calls from parents or the recommendation from the principal to be on some committee or something." Have you ever made this shift? What happens when a teacher becomes more internally directed?

4. Laurie claims that she speaks differently to each audience and in each situation, yet her message does not change because she works to stay connected to her core values and her core does not change. How do you explain this paradoxical claim of change and stability? What does it suggest about the power of integrity and being internally directed?

5. When Laurie was in crisis, she learned a core principle of jujitsu: "Instead of catching the sword when it comes at you, a master will spin and stand next to the person rather than in opposition to the person. That made so much sense to me and categorically changed the way I approached colleagues from that point on. If I don't agree with you, we find out why. I stand here [to the side]. If there is a kid whom I'm combating in class, I don't try to catch their sword. I stand here instead [to the side]." This suggests that Laurie learned new ways to transform conflict into cooperation. Why do empowered people tend to learn how to turn conflict into cooperation, and why is it important?

GROWING YOUR PRACTICE

1. Think about the four dimensions of empowerment: meaning, competence, self-determination, and impact. Which one would you highlight as a strength? Which would you consider a weakness? Identify a practice in this chapter (or a practice stimulated by this chapter) that you could experiment with this week in your classroom.

2. Laurie's web activity is a powerful practice that serves as the template for how she wants her classroom to operate. Identify a core activity or lesson that sets the tone for your classroom. How does it integrate the quadrants of the Connect Framework?

   ■ Yellow quadrant (relationships)

   ■ Green quadrant (continuous improvement)

   ■ Blue quadrant (high expectations)

   ■ Red quadrant (stable environment)

   Identify one or two ways in which you can continue to leverage and build on this practice to make it even more powerful.

CHAPTER 6

Empowering Others:
Teaching That Transforms

And as we let our own light shine, we unconsciously give other people permission to do the same. As we are liberated from our fear, our presence automatically liberates others.

— Marianne Williamson
A Return to Love

VICKI IS A VETERAN FOURTH-GRADE TEACHER IN A SUBURBAN SCHOOL district. For her the most rewarding aspect of teaching is the results. But she is not talking about test scores. As Vicki explains, "It's more the results of the change in students themselves and the growth in confidence....Over the year you just see them blossom from timid or being afraid to try, to a 'bring it on' type attitude."

Vicki then shared an example from the previous school year. On the first day of school, she announced that it was time to begin math. Suddenly, a student named Ella burst into tears. Vicki took Ella into the hall for a private conversation. As they talked the young girl shared, "I can't do math. Numbers don't make sense to me. I hate math."

Vicki made Ella a promise. "You know what? You don't know me very well, and I don't know you very well yet, but I'm going to trust that you are a mathematician. You just haven't figured it out yet, and I need you to trust that I can get you to see that."

As the year unfolded, Vicki connected with Ella: "I worked with her to go back and build some foundations, hence confidence that she could kind of start moving on." Vicki began to see positive changes. "She was still intimidated, but she was no longer crying and would attempt many of the problems with assistance." Near the end of the first grading period, Vicki experienced another breakthrough. Ella approached her after class and said, "I kind of like this math stuff!"

At the end of the year, Ella shared that math was her favorite subject and that she "loved the challenge of trying to figure it out." She scored at an accelerated level on the state math assessment and wrote a letter to thank Vicki for turning her into a mathematician.

A Unique Interpretation

Vicki had a unique perspective about helping Ella embrace mathematics, one that goes beyond directive assumptions about teaching. She told us that she did not turn Ella into a mathematician. She told us that Ella always was a mathematician. What kept the girl from knowing that she was a mathematician was her lack of confidence and a poor foundation in some basic skills. Once Ella developed those skills and experienced some success, her confidence blossomed. What was already inside her simply came out.

Another HET told us that her goal is to get her students to appreciate and love learning. Yet students come to her with many self-imposed limitations that have to be "pushed away before they can actually understand the content." Like Ella, many students come to school full of fears and doubts that diminish their ability to learn.

The root word for education is *educe,* which means "to bring out of." Like Vicki, many HETs emphasize bringing out the best in their students. Vicki sees potential where others may not and finds ways to draw it out of her students so that they can, as Marianne Williamson suggests, "let their own light shine." In other words, a student's level of empowerment is related to the rate at which he or she will learn.

CHAPTER OVERVIEW

Empowering Others

In this chapter we use Vicki's story to suggest that HETs are transformational leaders who build an empowering classroom culture. In this culture students are more likely to become self-empowered learners who engage themselves in their own learning process. As described in chapter 5, people who are self-empowered experience an increase in meaning, competence, autonomy, and impact. We build on the previous chapter on teacher empowerment by proposing ways that teachers can transform their students into self-empowered learners who take initiative and become more confident.

Transformational Teaching

Vicki is a transformational teacher.[1] In the corporate world, transformational leaders can be identified by a telltale sign: their direct reports tend to be leaders as well. HETs like Vicki tend to have a similar effect on their students. Transformational leaders believe that others can change and grow. They have this belief because they have experienced deep change and the resulting transformation of their own potential. They recognize potential in others because they see potential in themselves. So, they lead in ways that promote deep change in others. Teachers like Vicki empower their students because they themselves are empowered.

Vicki is trying not only to empower students individually but also to build an organization that is empowering. She indicates that she is trying to build an organization that is an "avenue for success," a place where her students' potential is realized, where learning targets are mastered while her students simultaneously thrive: "If it's the only place in their life that is a positive force, then hopefully they can see that it's worth the investment." She is trying to build an organization of higher purpose that supports transformative learning experiences.

RESEARCH FOUNDATIONS

Transformational Leadership

Transformational leaders place less (but not zero) emphasis on the red quadrant of the Connect Framework (e.g., hierarchical control) and increase the emphasis on the other three quadrants. In the organizations they construct, influence is less tied to position, thereby allowing more leadership at all levels of an organization. In the classroom, teachers and students share leadership. Transformational leadership is reflected in the four kinds of behavior described below.[2]

- **Idealized influence.** Transformational leaders operate with moral power. They model high standards of ethical and moral conduct (red quadrant). They do things that gain respect, build trust, and increase the willingness to believe. This may result in higher-quality relationships (yellow quadrant).

- **Inspirational motivation.** Transformational leaders provide collective meaning by articulating an appealing, inspiring vision, offering challenging standards and communicating optimism. This may result in a shared vision and the emergence of a collective purpose (yellow and blue quadrants). One way that the HETs we interviewed inspire action is by simultaneously building confidence and providing challenge. They teach to stimulate growth as well as to perform on the test.

- **Intellectual stimulation.** Transformational leaders challenge assumptions, take risks, and solicit input from followers. They value learning and encourage independent thinking and creative outcomes. This may facilitate the desire for and the emergence of knowledge generation (green quadrant). An intellectually stimulating leader is one who helps followers think in new ways. The leader helps people reexamine their own assumptions, look for new perspectives, and consider different ways to think about a problem.

- **Individualized consideration.** Transformational leaders act as respectful mentors or coaches. They listen and attend to individual needs. They provide empathy and support, emphasize the need for respect, and celebrate the contributions of each person. This may lead to the emergence of intrinsic motivation (yellow quadrant). Specifically, HETs tend to envision a family context, commit to the common good, tend to individual needs, and provide support.

Building an Empowering Culture

In the previous chapters, we heard several ways to describe the "magic" that unfolds when teachers and their students are at their best. Diana used the phrase "the living beast" to describe the magical chemistry that sometimes emerges in her classroom. Aaron spoke of a "different realm" in which his students are pushing him and they are creating knowledge together. For Sarah these kinds of experiences create "an energy" that she can see and feel as "everyone's brainwaves are making connections." Vicki has her own way of talking about this experience. She told us the classroom becomes "electric" as students engage in lively discussions and respectful debates.

Notice that none of these teachers talks about the exhilaration of standing at the front of the room, delivering a powerful lecture. We did not hear those kinds of stories. The experiences these teachers describe emerged when students become empowered participants in their own learning. In the words of another HET, her goal is "to set this classroom on fire and get a good conversation going." Many HETs indicated that they put a lot of thought and effort into building a culture that nurtures these kinds of learning experiences.

At the beginning of this chapter, we shared an account of Vicki interacting with a student who "knew" she could not do math. Ella's assumptions about her ability to do math were based on her previous experiences in math class. For Ella to become a confident mathematician, she had to make new assumptions about her own capabilities.

Recall what Vicki told her: "You don't know me very well, and I don't know you very well yet, but I'm going to trust that you are a mathematician. You just haven't figured it out yet, and I need you to trust that I can get you to see that." This is not only a sensitive statement that builds trust (yellow quadrant) but also a visionary statement (green quadrant). Vicki was enticing Ella into experiences that changed her sense of herself and allowed her to become a more empowered person.

Culture-Building as Powerful Practice for Empowering Students

Vicki works across the four quadrants of the framework to nurture an empowering learning environment (see figure 6.1). She is a woman with

Figure 6.1 *Culture-Building as a Powerful Practice*

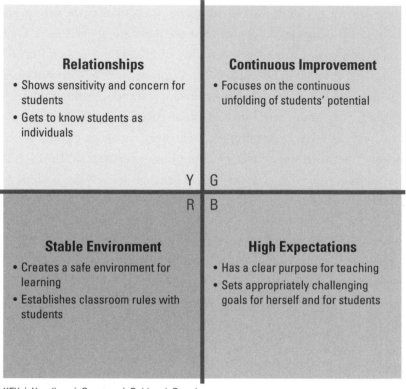

KEY | Y: yellow | G: green | B: blue | R: red

clarity of purpose. She loves teaching. Yet teaching, for Vicki, is not really about the content. The content is a great tool for reaching her higher purpose, which is the continuous unfolding of her students' potential.

To unleash the potential in her students, Vicki has to relate to them in a certain way. As we saw in her exchange with Ella, Vicki shows sensitivity, concern, and the ability to build trust. She believes that it is important to get to know her students as individuals: "You have to learn who this little person is that you are trying to grow because if you don't know their needs, you can't grow them."

Many of Vicki's students come from difficult home situations. She tries to create a safe environment where students can "engage in the day" and escape from reality for a while. At the beginning of each year, she and her students collaboratively decide on the rules that will allow her classroom to become "a place of opportunities for all." She also invites students to leave a note on her desk if they would like to discuss something personal, and she will arrange to have lunch with them or talk with them one-on-one. Vicki comments, "You just [have to] be there. You try to be what they need for the short time that you have them."

While Vicki is full of compassion for her students, she also has high expectations for them. She constantly assesses herself and her students to ensure that she is providing the appropriate amount of challenge. She does not hesitate to push: "I have high expectations for me, and I work hard every year to raise the bar…for them. Once we meet a goal, we're not done. We raise it a little higher, and we raise it a little higher, and I try to do the same for myself."

Vicki made another complex statement: "I always teach to the top, but I'm on all levels, making sure that I'm not only teaching the ones that appear to be ready to be there because I think they can all be there."

Vicki also has high expectations for her students' behavior. She addresses red quadrant discipline issues directly while maintaining sensitivity and respect for each child (yellow quadrant).

TEACHER'S TIP

Vicki: Students who have particular issues with discipline and self-control are treated with the same respect as their peers. One-on-one lunches are often a medium for candid discussion and goal setting. A common question I ask is "What do you need from me to help you make better choices and to be more successful?"

Acquiring Attractive Power

The Research Foundations box earlier in this chapter describes the four behaviors associated with transformational influence. The concern that Vicki shows to her students is an illustration of individual consideration. Her orientation toward high standards and continuous challenge connects her students to a desirable future and is an illustration of inspirational motivation. In this section we focus on a behavior that is sometimes more difficult to understand.

When we asked Vicki to explain why students, like Ella, are willing to work so hard in class, she told us:

> I've given them everything I have to offer. You know, I think the school year is extremely rewarding, but it is exhausting because you just give everything. It's not just academics....I think I'm trying to give them the best of me. Like the best person I know how to be, character traits that I either have or am working to acquire or to polish. So I just don't think you can look at them [students] as a statistic, as a score. You know, you've got to look at the whole person.

In this statement Vicki reveals assumptions about influence that go beyond the directive perspective. The directive perspective assumes that power derives from physical strength, expertise, hierarchical position, and social influence. Vicki suggests an additional source of power; she believes that the process of learning is influenced by her own character or integrity. She is concerned not only about her character but also about the character traits she is trying to refine or new traits she is trying to develop. She believes that constantly becoming a better person is necessary to her success. She is concerned not only with who she is but also with who she is trying to become. She is concerned with presenting the best version of herself.

⬤ *TEACHER'S TIP*

Vicki: I truly believe that my values as a teacher are a direct result of the values I established over time as I grew up. I still live by many of the rules of my childhood.

- You have an opportunity for a great and fulfilling life, and it is up to you to climb the ladder from which you can acquire it.

- Ask for help only when really needed.

- If you fall off the horse, get up, dust yourself off, and, most importantly,...get back on and hold the reins a little tighter.

- Mistakes that are genuine hold great promise for learning.

- If you do not have something nice to think or say about a person, take your blinders off and look again. If you still don't, pray that the other person is not as closed-minded as you are choosing to be.

These principles represent the push for excellence that was in every fiber of my developing years. The ability to accept rigor and challenges, self-evaluate, and be resourceful develops independence and strong character. It is the very core of who you are and what you do.

Research supports this view of power and influence.[3] Transformational leaders form relationships with followers in which inspiration flows both ways. The leader and the followers become entwined in an emergent process. They lift each other with positive influence and move to higher levels of performance. Perceptions, assumptions, and expectations become aligned with the pursuit of the common good. The organization becomes a learning organization. The members become more intrinsically motivated.

The process begins as leaders build relationships of trust, respect, and admiration. One factor at the heart of this process is integrity—moral power, or what researchers call idealized influence (see the Research Foundations box). This kind of power is not coercive. It is attractive. The leader serves as a role model. Followers are emotionally, cognitively, and behaviorally attracted to the leader. They want to be like the leader, so over time they emulate and internalize the ideals of the leader.

Vicki is implying that her students respond not only to what they hear her say but also based on how they feel. These feelings determine whether they identify with and want to be like her. A teacher who is working to be the best person she can be is a teacher who is using moral power or idealized influence to attract students to be the best students they can be.

🖋 *TEACHER'S TIP*

Vicki: You can't be afraid to say, "You know what, I goofed. You know what, I made a mistake, or you know what, I wasn't happy with yesterday. Not that I'm not happy with you—I'm not happy with the way I approached this lesson. I want to redo it today." It shows students that you are not going to settle for less than your best. When that is your class motto for them, you have got to live it also.

The education literature is becoming more focused on the importance of students' character development.[4] Vicki's comments suggest that there should be a similar interest in the character development of teachers. Focusing on character traits aids the process of bringing out the best teacher in you and empowering the best learner in your students.

In the remainder of this chapter, we propose ways that teachers can help students move from fear and self-doubt to adaptive confidence. Students become more self-empowered as they find meaning, develop competence, experience autonomy, and recognize the impact that they can have on the world. Figure 6.2 summarizes the shifts students make to become self-empowered learners.

Figure 6.2 *Transforming Students into Self-Empowered Learners*

	Directive Perspective	**Co-creative Perspective**
Meaning	Extrinsically motivated	Intrinsically motivated
Competence	Limited by self-doubt	Elevated by self-belief
Autonomy	Controlled	Self-directed
Impact	Limited power	Powerful

Finding Meaning

Vicki, like the other teachers in this book, firmly believes that "all kids can be successful. You just have to find the way to reach them." She further explains, "I see it over and over and over [when] you believe in them and you're invested in their success." She describes her role as being part salesperson, and each day she strives to get both her students and their parents to "buy into the value of education." Vicki believes that education is about more than test results; it is about the future and the self-satisfaction that expands in a student who is pushing toward his or her potential. For Vicki the process of pushing toward potential is never ending. Vicki wants her students to see a larger meaning in the work they do together in class.

Another HET told us that students have gifts that they do not know about. The teacher's job is to find out about the student's natural strengths and create conditions in which the student might dare to exercise those gifts. She said, "I think empowerment has to do with love, and it has to do with passion. And it has to do with finding that one thing in your life that you want to pursue—that goal that you might have—and setting up a plan of how you're going to get there."

This teacher is articulating a theory of practice. Her theory suggests that just as teachers excel when they find purpose, students will also excel as they find their purpose. Students need to be both challenged (blue quadrant) and supported (yellow quadrant). They need to be led into acting in ways that will allow them to experience their best selves.

Another HET shared an example of the payoff that can come from tapping into her students' passions:

> One of my students has always said she wants to go into fashion as a career because she loves fashion, accessories, and makeup and that she has no interest in science. A couple of weeks ago, we were studying stoichiometry in class, and I was talking to my students about how most industrial manufacturers hire chemists who use stoichiometry to calculate and maximize product yields. A few days later, that student told me that she was at Sephora, her favorite makeup

store, when she realized that she wanted to become a chemist and work for Sephora to test and improve their products and their yields. She was extremely excited about it and told me that she would take AP [advanced placement] chemistry next year for that purpose. And I realized that this is one of my favorite things about teaching: helping students realize that chemistry is everywhere around them, helping them find connections between what they love and science, and getting them excited and motivated to learn science.

Teachers like Vicki see their role as larger than teaching students the required content. They instill the value of education in their students and help them find meaning in their schoolwork.

Challenge and Support

The HETs we interviewed tend to see potential in everyone, so they work with each child to communicate high expectations and rigorous standards. They teach with a sense of urgency. Not a moment is wasted. Many, like Vicki, move at a pace designed for the highest-level students. These teachers constantly challenge students to leave their comfort zones while providing them the support they need to stretch to these challenges. Many teachers told us that as students develop a sense of security and trust, it becomes possible to push them. But the process takes time.

These teachers describe integrating challenge (blue quadrant) and support (yellow quadrant), recognizing the complexity of doing so. Students must be pushed—but not too far. Many HETs provided examples of this kind of integration. For example, one HET told us, "All of my students know that they must give me their very best. From day one of the school year, we practice daily expectations and behaviors." This HET claimed that she is consistent in her expectations throughout the school year, and she lets her students know that she will not be disappointed so long as they give their best effort. She also nurtures their commitment: "My students are like my family. They know I love them and want the best for them."

Another HET provided this example of working with students across varying ability levels:

I teach to the very highest level. With the middle group, I find that they try to stretch to the highest level. And with the low group, I make modifications, but I don't let them grovel on their level. I kind of pull them up and have higher expectations than probably they are comfortable [with]. I try to bring every child up to that point where they are slightly uncomfortable but not over the top. I don't want to push them over the dam, but I want them to be slightly uncomfortable in the learning process so that it's not easy for them, that they are always struggling and striving.

These teachers describe bringing students to the edge of discomfort while instilling the confidence that they can succeed.

Elevated Outcomes

As teachers like Vicki integrate challenge and support, students are more likely to find goals for which they are willing to work hard. We heard many stories of this transformation. Vicki provides an example of the impact this can have on a student. The parents of one of her students contacted her with a request. They asked Vicki to tutor their son because he seemed to value what Vicki had to say more than he valued what they had to say. They were having ongoing problems at home, so they also asked Vicki to meet with them and their son. They met for two hours to discuss the difference between the way the boy behaved at home and at school.

In our interview we asked Vicki to explain the difference observed by the parents. She responded, "Expectations…I expect him to be tremendous, but I'm also there to help him along the way to get there."

This story illustrates transformational influence in action. Transformational leaders, mentors, and teachers orient toward the best in people, and they build relationships and communities that help realize this potential. They expect their people to be tremendous, and their people rise to the expectation.

In a transactional culture, managers—or, as in Vicki's story, parents—may see people as problems to be solved. In conventional logic a problem tends to be something to be acted on and eliminated. When people are seen as problems, the potential for empowerment drops dramatically. They are unlikely to become their best.

This particular boy was seen as a problem at home and as tremendous at school. He was living in two different cultures. In each culture he enacted a different self. In each culture he learned differently.

There is another contrast that is helpful to note. One teacher, whose students typically had average learning gains, told us that she expects her students to respect her. Then she told us, "I try to respect them back as long as they warrant it." This statement is based on conventional notions of justice, and it fits the conventional assumptions of social exchange. Unfortunately, this approach generates a reactive strategy. Students are respected only if they are respectful.

Some of our interviewees spoke of giving unconditional positive regard. This is another example of powerful practice. For example, one HET described correcting a disrespectful student (blue quadrant) while showing complete respect for the student (yellow quadrant). Acting on such an assumption is a proactive strategy. A person who is corrected while also receiving complete respect is much more likely to stay engaged in learning than a person who is simply being corrected.

Developing Competence

Empowered teachers act with a sense of competence, and they seek to develop the same sense in their students. They typically do this by building relationships of trust and getting their students to engage in the process. They often talk about "small wins."

Aaron, whom you met in chapter 3, told us that when students say they do not like math, what they really mean is that their past experience leads them to believe that they are not good at math. This means that they have developed assumptions or beliefs about themselves. The directive strategy of trying to talk them out of such beliefs is not likely to be effective.

An alternative strategy is to engage students in experiences that challenge their self-defeating assumptions. Aaron explained, "When you can begin to build some success into those students, they tend to change their opinion about what they like. People like what they are good at, and they don't like things that are difficult for them and that make them feel stupid."

Here learning is not only about content. It is also about feelings, self-perceptions, and the development of virtue and character. As we have seen, Vicki emphasizes the development of character traits. She told us that at the beginning of the year there is one character trait she emphasizes: "Perseverance is huge for me because that's usually what I find that interferes with success and confidence. [Students] don't have the stamina to stick with it, and they throw in the towel easily. And if those things are present, then I usually try to tackle those first. We have a lot of class discussions about perseverance."

Vicki also helps her students learn to persevere by modeling those behaviors for them: "I think first you have to live it. You have to define it. You have to be a model of perseverance."

She shares personal examples of carrying on in the face of difficulty. She helps her students to understand the benefits that accrue from "building stamina and perseverance and other habits."

Kelli, whom we met in chapter 1, also spoke to us about the importance of modeling and character development: "You have to know how to speak to one another; you have to know how to think; you have to know how to problem-solve; you have to have an attitude that you'll never give up.... That attitude's important, and those things, I can demonstrate those for you, and I can model those for you, and I can encourage those things in you, and I can maybe even start to teach you those things."

Like Vicki, another HET spent the entire year nurturing a girl who felt she was incapable of doing math. Toward the end of the year, the student took a particularly difficult quiz and got every answer right:

> She was, I think, one of the only ones in the class who got every single question right, and it was kind of like that light bulb moment where I think she finally started to see herself as an intelligent being and that she could do it. It was after that I saw her sit up a little bit more. I saw her answer questions a little bit more. I try to catch the kids being successful at some topic....I want to catch them being

successful so that they have more confidence in themselves; and once they have more confidence in themselves doing math, then they want to do it more.

This experience changed how the student saw herself. Her success allowed her to display a new, more competent identity.

⬤ *TEACHER'S TIP*

Vicki: One change in my practice over the past 10 years has been to do more frontloading of key concepts. I do a lot of immersion into a subject before the actual formal teaching part of it. For example, if I'm going to do division, by the time I get to division, students have already been exposed to it 50 times. They just don't realize that they have been kind of picking it up along the way before we formally get to where I'm using it as a focus.

Focus on Learning: Building Competency

Given the emphasis on building competence and providing challenge, we were surprised by a trend in the interviews. We had some expectation that teachers with high value-added scores might emphasize the importance of tests. Instead many HETs make claims such as "I do not teach to the test."

This does not mean that they ignore testing. It means that they place more emphasis on learning. The teachers who made such statements tend to believe that if they are doing what they are "supposed to be doing," that is, stimulating progress and helping students acquire both cognitive and emotional capacity, the test scores naturally follow. Vicki elaborated on these ideas: "I don't worry about test scores because I think those are the icing on the cake. If I take care of what I'm supposed to be doing, I feel like they'll rise to the occasion."

Rather than allowing themselves to be pulled into the narrow focus of the test preparation world, teachers like Vicki work to get their students out of their comfort zones and into the struggle of moving one step forward. Their challenge is to keep students moving forward.

Experiencing Autonomy

In the end the process of empowerment requires that people take charge of their own lives. They have to become self-directed. They have to make their own decisions. Vicki described a significant shift in her approach to teaching: "I used to do…some of the extrinsic type rewards, and this was probably about 15 years ago. It dawned on me that if they're working for the sticker…they're not working for themselves. And at that point, what they do loses value….They're not doing the work for the sake of self-growth. They're doing it to get that sticker or a piece of candy or something else."

With this realization Vicki immediately pulled all of the extrinsically oriented rewards out of her classroom. It was a difficult adjustment for both Vicki and her students. As she thought about why she originally started using those types of rewards, she commented, "I think you just want to see them smile" and to encourage them to "keep trying," but at some point she felt like she had crossed the line. Vicki began to work toward building intrinsic motivation because intrinsically motivated students are more likely to develop a sense of autonomy.

Some teachers, especially beginning teachers, may struggle to gain control of their classrooms. The notion of surrendering control may be the furthest thing from their minds. Like Sarah in chapter 4, they may fear that "the wheels would come off and [the] classroom would explode." The very notion of surrendering control to students violates the conventional assumptions of hierarchy.

Many of the teachers we meet in this book are aware of the directive assumptions around control. As Kelli told us, "Traditionally school is not a place where students have a voice. It's where you come and have things done to you. You sit and get. I'm not interested in sit and get. I didn't 'get' very well as a student because all I did was sit."

Kelli is not interested in telling. She is anxious for her students to have ownership and their own voices. She wants them to "have a say in how much you learn, how fast you learn, and the ways in which you learn it." She further explains, "It's a dialogue between us, and we're going to figure out that journey and we're going to take that journey together."

From Teacher-Centered to Student-Centered: Promoting Autonomy

The process of surrendering control and giving students a sense of autonomy is not straightforward. It is dynamic and complex. Vicki described how this process unfolds in her classroom: "I always tell the kids, 'I'm going to hold both reins today. We're driving wild horses and I'm going to hold both reins.' And then on the day that I'm kind of putting them in a cooperative group, I'm telling them, 'Okay, I'm giving you a rein today, but if you scare me to death, I'm taking it back.' And then when they're independent, then it's like, okay, 'You've got both reins. Hold on to those horses.'"

In surrendering control to her students, Vicki does not abdicate her responsibility for their learning. This was also true of Laurie, whom we met in chapter 5, who told her students, "Can you sit down on the floor and go through this again? Because on one hand, we are equal, but I am still in charge. I know what I'm doing. Where have I let you down so far?"

Vicki constantly assesses her students' readiness to take on more ownership of their learning. She looks for evidence, such as when students are asking questions for clarification and naturally extending ideas through rich conversation. Vicki told us that she has to "feel comfortable that I've done my part to get them to the point where they can be successful and move into that next stage of kind of semi-independence and then on to being independent." She is fully present, monitoring and supporting their progress. If students get off track, she is ready to step in and redirect them.

Perhaps the greatest barrier to moving students toward autonomy is the identity of the teacher. A teacher may enjoy being the center of attention. Moving from teacher-centered teaching to learning-centered teaching is a shift that requires a change in perspective. One of our interviewees talked about this shift at length:

> I think it kind of goes back to that center of attention and not needing to be the one to tell everybody what's the right thing to do. In this case, letting the kids become more the focal point in your classroom because it is their classroom....In my classroom I do try to do a lot of things where they [students] have choice as to how they're going

to present an idea. They have a plethora of decisions that they can make. How do I best want to show what the theme of that story was? It's not me telling them what they have to do to show me that they understand and to show their classmates that they understand. So, [it's] giving them that choice and letting them, with my guidance, facilitate themselves....What's your plan? What's your goal? What do you want to show us in the end? What do you want to teach us? Letting them make some of those decisions. And I think that kind of does wean the teacher away from being that center of attention, and I think kids respond to that more.

These teachers are sharing their implicit theories of facilitation. Most developed their operating theory from experimentation. Through trial and error, they navigated the very difficult terrain of experiential learning. The shift from the directive role of instructor to the more co-creative role of facilitator is a deep change, a shift in identity. It is a shift that allows the teacher to empower others.

◑ TEACHER'S TIP

Vicki: At the end of the day, I choose five students, and I sit down and reflect over the day. *Are they asking questions? Do I have to initiate?* So it is more than just *Did they get the math concept* or *Did they understand government?* It is *Are they participating?* Especially when students are working in small groups or with partners, I reflect on what I observed. *Did they sit back and kind of follow along or were they actively participating?* In a partnership I look for two leaders, not one, and I try to grow the ones who do not step up.

Recognizing Impact

From what we have learned about Vicki, it is easy to see her as an innately gifted teacher who never has problems, but that is not the case.

Vicki told us a story that resembles Kelli's story about learning to become the key to every door. The previous year was one of Vicki's most challenging as a teacher. She began to lose confidence and wonder if she had chosen the right career after all. She was having difficulty moving the class forward and motivating her students to learn. She was stuck. The challenge led Vicki to try a new strategy: "I believe the turning point came when I moved from normal teaching strategies to teaching from the heart. We began having heart-to-heart conversations in the form of class meetings to discuss what I could and could not do for them and setting goals for what they had to do for themselves. I believe it was the candid, and sometimes difficult, conversations that led to the positive changes."

As these discussions continued, a subgroup of students began to experience things in a whole different light. They started to find the learning process enjoyable, and the class changed. Vicki told us, "I was reminded that we teach so much more than subjects....We teach children."

Although Vicki is a veteran teacher, a new group of students brought a new set of challenges. The techniques and the approaches that she had relied on in the past were not working, and Vicki's assumptions about teaching and learning were challenged by this failure, so she tried a new way of relating with her students (yellow quadrant). Vicki set boundaries (red quadrant) for what she "could and could not do," and helped her students set goals so that they could move forward independently (blue quadrant). Her experiments (green quadrant) resulted in new assumptions, and new behaviors emerged. The unengaged students began to engage.

Like the teachers in the previous chapters, Vicki experienced greater success with her students when she stopped relying on the assumptions that were based on her past experiences and instead embraced the reality of her present experiences that required her to grow. To do this Vicki had to become more vulnerable, and she engaged her students in authentic conversations about their learning. By transforming herself, she became a more complex and capable person. She was doing what she wanted her students to do. Attracted by her moral power, they were more willing to engage their own present reality, and they began to take more ownership of their learning.

Vicki's students changed after she first changed herself. The directive, hierarchical perspective assumes that students are supposed to respond to authority figures who tell them how they should be changing. Yet we've all experienced circumstances in which an authority figure told us what to do and we resisted. In the co-creative perspective, the class is a network of interrelated people who have autonomy and choice. The objective is not to limit their autonomy but to continually increase it. The strategy is to attract them to better, more moral choices. This attraction is partially created by modeling moral power. The teacher attracts the students to be the best student in them again and again.

It is natural for most of us to doubt a strategy that relies on moral power. Teachers, for example, may point to their most challenging students and explain that they are difficult to impact because their lives feel out of control. Nearly every aspect of their lives is difficult. It is normal to encounter students like this and conclude that it is unrealistic to expect them to take ownership of their learning. The HETs we interviewed see these students differently. One told us of her experience with such a student: "She seems to care about nothing, and she is very difficult to motivate." The teacher elaborated:

> I just talked to her yesterday about what she could change. I said, "Can you change anything that's going on at home?" She said "No." And I said, "No, you can't, and I'm sorry about that. But what can you change? What can you do? What can you affect?" And so we talked about how she could change personally—what she does and how she reacts to her circumstances and what she does with what she has. And I felt just a little positive light after that conversation yesterday, and she started trying.

This is a statement of powerful practice. It is a statement of challenge (blue quadrant) and support (yellow quadrant). It is an analysis of existing constraints (red quadrant) and of future potential (green quadrant). The teacher is not only using words. She is also providing a model of empowerment. She is using moral power to attract her student into new life patterns.

Another teacher told us, "Regardless of what's going on around them, [students] are in control of what they do with that and where they go from here. And you know, they can take that situation and make it whatever they want it to be....They have the opportunity to impact and change their situation, maybe not immediately and maybe not everything, but they have some control over how they respond to it."

As you think back on your own childhood, you may recall many times when you felt like you had no say in what you did or where you went. At school you were likely told when to arrive, where to sit, and what to learn. Like Kelli, you may have felt like you did not have a voice. Indeed today, in a world where so many things come at a teacher from outside the classroom door, it is not surprising that some might feel that they have little voice. In all of these stories, we see HETs helping students find the voice that many teachers may lack. One way they do this is by helping students take responsibility for the things they can control. When students realize that they have a voice, they may even begin to exercise it outside the classroom.

Learning to Be Change Agents

In chapter 5 you met Laurie, who spoke of the importance of learning her students' voices and of teaching them to express their own authentic voices "so that they know what they're saying, why they're saying it, to whom they're saying it [and] for what purposes."

Similarly, Vicki sees great value in teaching her students how to express themselves effectively. She not only supports and challenges her students but also teaches them to do the same. She told us, "I am a firm believer that teachers need to model, practice, and expect honest and respectful challenges—presented to and encouraged between students— for the common good and for evaluation of self and peers." For example, she teaches students to say things like "I appreciate your ideas. Have you thought about this?" The simple question is simultaneously supportive and challenging.

Vicki's students are learning the skills of transformational influence, which they can apply outside her classroom. Vicki described one incident when she went to pick up her class from the gym. As she did she heard one of her students telling the gym teacher: "I respectfully would like to challenge your decision on not allowing us to play such and such next week." This illustration returns us to the words of Marianne Williamson: "As we let our own light shine, we unconsciously give other people permission to do the same."

⬤ *TEACHER'S TIP*

Vicki: I think probably the most fun I have with students is when we get into a debate. A lot of times it is over the analysis of literature, and we will go to the carpet and have a round-robin conversation. We end up in two lines facing off, and their job is to convince the other side. They have to have evidence—it can't just be some wild idea that they have—so they have to always come back to the text or come back to a parallel text that they can use to support their point of view. At some point we stop, and I say, "Think for a minute about what we've talked about. Is there anyone who would like to change sides?" And, inevitably, there is. Through these conversations we get to where I want them to get with the learning. But it is fourth grade. Teaching them to have those respectful debates is absolutely delightful to watch, to be a part of, and to facilitate. The growth that I see in their communication skills is absolutely amazing.

Summary

HETs are self-empowered individuals—they have a greater sense of personal meaning, competence, autonomy, and impact. The literature on transformational leaders provides some insight into how teachers like Vicki use their transformational influence to also empower their students. HETs entice their students to find their own meaning, develop confidence in their ability to learn, and find their own path forward to make a difference. The students of such teachers may learn at an accelerated rate. Consistent with the epigraph at the start of this chapter, through empowerment HETs allow their students to transcend their fears to let their own light shine.

PLANTING SEEDS

1. Vicki helped a student see the mathematician that was already within her but not yet realized. She supported the student to help her see the potential within her. What potential do you overlook in your own life or your students' lives? How can you nurture a sense of possibility?

2. Many HETs made the claim that they do not teach to the test. Instead they focus on learning. What does it mean to focus on learning instead of test scores? How can focusing too heavily on test scores (blue quadrant) get in the way of learning?

3. Empowering others often feels scary because we worry about losing control. Why do Vicki and the other teachers feel okay even as they share control with students to co-create the learning environment in their classrooms? How can you share more influence, power, or authority with your students or others in your life?

GROWING YOUR PRACTICE

1. Vicki simultaneously challenges and supports her students. She challenges them to get out of their comfort zones while providing a psychologically safe space to learn and grow. How can you help your students or others in your life to grow through challenge *and* support? Give one specific example and try it next week.

2. In this chapter we shared several stories of HETs who helped students develop a greater sense of intrinsic motivation and personal impact. Identify someone in your life on whom you have made a positive impact in a similar way. What factors do you think contributed to your success? Identify two or three strategies from this chapter or your own experiences that you can implement in your classroom to improve students' intrinsic motivation.

CHAPTER 7

A Process for Development: Embedding Self-Reflection

What's needed, in my view, is a perspective that allows us a fresh look at our most basic assumptions about teaching and learning, a perspective that takes nothing for granted and focuses on the simple but crucial questions of what works, what doesn't work, and why.

—Salman Khan
The One World Schoolhouse

MICHELLE IS A NO-NONSENSE HET WITH 14 YEARS OF EXPERIENCE. In addition to teaching high school English, she coaches the girls volleyball team. In the middle of the 2011–2012 school year, she and others joined us in a pilot program to improve the overall effectiveness of their teaching. The experience changed her.

The goal of the pilot was to apply what we had learned about HETs to catalyze and support teachers' professional growth. We asked HETs from several schools to form professional learning teams (PLTs) with three to five other educators at their schools. PLT members assessed their individual strengths and growth opportunities relative to the quadrants of the Connect Framework. The members then used this information to develop a professional growth plan that stretched their practice from an area of strength into an area of growth with the support of their peers.

The Reflect Assessment provides teachers with feedback on their strengths and growth areas relative to the framework (see Resource A at the back of the book). Michelle, like most of the teachers who participated in this first pilot, was not surprised by the results of this assessment. She already knew that her growth area would be in the yellow quadrant:

I used to think that whole rapport thing was overrated. I got along with my volleyball players and my athletes, and that was that.... I loved that perception of myself as rigorous and stern and strict.... I felt like I could look in the mirror and say, "My kids are growing. They're doing really good things academically." So when I took [the Reflect Assessment]…that just confirmed what I already knew. But this [pilot program] made me look at it and think, *Okay, so what's the big deal?* And I think I just kind of felt I have that reputation [of being intimidating], and I just felt like I didn't want that anymore.

Michelle wanted to maintain the high level of rigor in her classroom, but problems with a few of her students left her more open to making a change. After discussing the results of the Reflect Assessment with colleagues in her PLT, she decided to gather additional feedback from her students. She created a short survey that asked students to list the traits of those teachers who taught them well, who had a positive influence on them, and who were good role models. The results had a great impact on her: "I realized that many of the adjectives [my students] used didn't describe me. Let me tell you, that was a harsh realization for me. I shed some real tears over this. So, my vision of myself came crashing down.... I just had to reconcile that the teachers that kids were remembering, that they were saying, 'I remember the subject matter as well'…none of those described me."

The survey results were a jolt that challenged Michelle's sense of herself as a teacher. In the earlier chapters, we shared examples of life jolts triggered by external events. For Kelli it was advice from well-meaning colleagues. For Aaron it was a note from a student. In this chapter we share stories of teachers who jolted themselves into the process of deep change. We also share stories of teachers who made smaller, incremental changes to their practice. The pilot program taught us that even highly effective teachers can benefit from paying closer attention to certain aspects of their practice.

While particular needs may vary, the Connect Framework provides a common language that helps teachers more clearly articulate those needs and engage in meaningful conversations with their peers about making changes in their practice. The framework also gives teachers a way to organize their thoughts and narrow the scope of their improvement efforts. In addition, the Reflect Assessment provides a basic measure of effective practice relative to the framework. Even though a majority of teachers could predict their results, seeing it quantified made it more difficult to downplay the underemphasized aspects of their practice.

CHAPTER OVERVIEW

A Process for Development

In this final chapter, we use Michelle's story to describe a professional development approach grounded in the Connect Framework and what we have learned from other highly effective teachers. This approach enables teachers at all levels to use the framework to recognize and leverage their strengths as well as identify their most fertile areas for growth. Ultimately, improved practice is a result of smart assessment, focused experimentation, collegial support, and systematic practice. This approach also allows teachers to interact with the assumptions that ground their practice and—if necessary—amend them in ways that allow them to be more effective.

Stretching Your Practice

The next phase of the pilot required teachers to move from awareness to action. As one HET commented after participating in the pilot, "There's a big difference between saying, 'I know I have to improve' and acting on it." For Michelle that meant creating a growth plan to stretch her practice into the yellow quadrant by improving her rapport with her students. As she did, she used her strengths in goal setting (blue quadrant) and management (red quadrant) to help her. She initially focused on the five students with whom she felt she had the poorest relationships. Michelle paid closer attention to her own behavior, including her body language, tone of voice, and how she communicated her high expectations to them: "I changed about four different things about my interaction with them because I knew I could control that. And that's what I reflected on. One day might have been just all about that kid, the next day might have been all about this kid, and just how things started to change."

Over time Michelle broadened her focus. She started monitoring her reactions to students "who need[ed] help, needed extra time outside the school day, and needed more than I could give them in class." She took notes about both her positive and negative interactions with students. Each week she continued to meet with her PLT to share her progress and struggles and to get feedback.

After three months, Michelle noticed positive changes in her class-room. Students became more willing to approach her and engage with her in class. For example, Michelle was pleased with her students' responses to her request that they read the newspaper and bring in articles that related to the class: "More and more I've been getting kids bringing me things from the newspaper, not because they have to in any way, shape, or form. Like we're reading George Orwell right now. There was some-thing in the paper Sunday that used the term *Orwellian,* and [a student] brought it in....And that wouldn't probably have happened earlier in the year because it was like "she scares me" kind of thing. But to me that's a measure that I can't put a number on."

Even more significant to Michelle were the unsolicited e-mails she received from the parents of two of the five students on whom she had been focusing. Unlike the typical parent e-mails that contain questions or concerns, these messages shared the positive things the students were saying at home about their recent experiences in Michelle's classroom.

Engaging in this work also had an uplifting effect on Michelle. While in some years she felt like she was just trying to make it to the end of the school year, Michelle noticed that she had a "bit more energy" during the final months of the school year and was saddened at the thought of losing this group of students "in part because of how well we are now functioning as a group." Michelle's stretch into the yellow quadrant produced a signifi-cant shift in her classroom culture without having a negative impact on her rigor or students' learning. At the end of the year, her students again demonstrated above-expected academic growth.

Increasing Teacher Effectiveness

While this first pilot taught us a lot about the conditions and the supports that are needed to facilitate professional growth, most of our participants were HETs meeting in small teams with other HETs. One of the questions that we frequently hear is "Can other teachers be taught to be highly effective?" If professional development is delivered through directive methods, the answer is probably no. Teachers will likely benefit only minimally. Reading this book, learning about the Connect Framework, and completing self-assessments are all excellent ways to learn about effective practice and to gain greater insight into your own teaching practice, but these things, by themselves, are insufficient.

Athletes do not improve their performance by being told to run faster, jump higher, or throw farther. Organizations do not expand their profits by merely understanding that they need to increase sales and cut costs. Similarly, teaching practice does not improve with the knowledge that we need to become more "blue" or more "yellow." Like Michelle, we may already know where we need to stretch our practice. Growth is a product of sustained effort, focus, and practice within a supportive environment that enables us to persist in these activities.

The challenge is to put yourself in circumstances that promote growth, but few organizations have created the infrastructure to support this kind of ongoing development. Often evaluation systems focus on identifying and intervening with the lowest performers while simply giving a stamp of approval to those who meet or exceed expectations. Fortunately, we already have excellent models of how to facilitate deep change. HETs create these conditions in their classrooms every day.

The question that we encourage educators to ask instead is "Can other teachers *learn to become* highly effective?" We believe that the answer to this question is yes. Current research suggests that people can become more effective leaders if they have the right kinds of new experiences and systematically reflect on those experiences.[1] They can learn their way into increased influence. If great teaching can be defined as transformational leadership, teachers can also learn their way into increased influence. Michelle is a prime example. She began to grow but not because of some external evaluation of her practice. Instead she became conscious of areas in which she needed to grow, and she leveraged her strengths to build capacities in those areas.

In this chapter we describe the work we are doing to support teachers' journeys to release the best teachers in themselves. Our work with teachers parallels the work that we are also doing to support leadership development in corporate, educational, and nonprofit settings. Great teachers and leaders are able to operate effectively in each dimension of the framework and to integrate practice across these dimensions. Although real development cannot be done *to* teachers and leaders, appropriately structured supports, tools, and resources can produce the conditions in which development is more likely to occur. Since our first pilot, we have worked with more diverse groups of teachers who have achieved similarly positive results. In the remainder of this chapter, we share some stories of their growth.

Supporting Professional Growth

How often have you attended a training session that felt disconnected and unrelated to the challenges you experience in your job? How many times have you participated in professional development that inspired you to try something new only to slip into old habits once you returned to work? Both scenarios likely left you feeling frustrated. In the first situation, you wasted valuable time listening to seemingly irrelevant information. In the second the information was valuable, but you had insufficient knowledge, motivation, and support to put it into action. In either case the information shared did little to promote professional growth.

Many teachers in our pilot program echoed this sentiment as they discussed their past experiences with professional development. For most of the teachers we worked with, the pilot was a completely different kind of professional development experience. Stephanie, for example, is a reading teacher who participated in our second pilot program during the 2012–2013 school year. According to her value-added scores going into the process, her students were making expected academic gains. Stephanie is like most teachers. She works hard to meet her students' needs, and at the end of the year her students show growth. But Stephanie wanted to find ways to accelerate her students' learning.

At the end of the pilot, Stephanie recounted how our approach to professional development was a new experience for her: "It is so empowering to be part of this [PLT] due to the fact that I got to choose what I wanted my project to be. No one came in and told me what I had to do. That was something I am not used to, and I liked that freedom."

After Stephanie decided which aspect of her practice to focus on, her PLT was there to ensure that she followed through with her plan. She reported, "The greatest benefit was designing a plan to help my students learn. I needed to be accountable for that, and this group empowered me to do so." During the pilot program, she met with her PLT weekly, and they listened, provided feedback, and supported her.

Increasing the Impact of Professional Learning

In education personalized learning is gaining momentum as a way to meet students' unique needs and aspirations. Personalization is a student-centered approach to learning in which the learning targets, methods, and pace are tailored to the abilities, interests, and needs of individual students.[2] It involves empowering learners by involving them in decisions about where, how, and what they learn. As we discussed in chapters 5 and 6, empowerment is central to the process of transformative learning. This approach also holds promise for improving how we develop professionally. If professional learning is to become more relevant, useful, and impactful, it should be personalized to recognize individual strengths and address individual developmental needs.

Recent research already supports this shift in focus. Monetary incentives and performance sanctions—characteristic of most standard evaluation and professional development systems—do little to move people toward exceptional performance. A more effective alternative is to create systems that treat educators as professionals and allow them to develop a greater sense of autonomy, mastery, and purpose.[3]

Our current work with teachers is designed to be empowering and intrinsically motivating. Our approach to professional learning applies what we have learned from HETs in such a way that educators experience significant growth along with:

- Increased autonomy in their choice of what to work on in their practice

- An increasing sense of competence and impact with respect to particular teaching practices

- A growing sense of meaning and purpose with respect to personalized learning[4]

We have evolved the pilot program into an approach called BFK•Connect that helps teachers assess their practice, develop core skills in underrepresented areas of their practice, and then integrate those new skills with the other dimensions of effectiveness.

BFK•Connect

BFK•Connect is a job-embedded approach to professional learning. Teachers use the Connect Framework and related tools and resources to more deeply examine their professional practice, develop a growth plan, and implement and monitor changes in their practice. In the words of one teacher, "The biggest thing I've learned in this experience has probably been that I don't need to reinvent myself....I have to take a look at what I'm already doing and ways to strengthen that. It's about balance."

Teachers begin this process by assessing their own practice relative to the Connect Framework and developing a plan to stretch their practice into dimensions that are currently underrepresented in their classrooms. As one teacher described it, this approach moves learning from "a single mold for all" to "a flexible and open opportunity to make your own mold for your own needs." Purpose builds as teachers connect their personal growth plan to specific changes in their classroom.

When talking about their strengths and weaknesses, teachers use terms like *stretch* and *grow* to describe the process of developing practices within a particular quadrant:

- "What this project has helped me to actualize is that I can use my strengths to grow into my weaknesses....It is in stretching strengths that weakness are not overcome, not compensated, but developed."

- ◼ "It's not about leaving one area to go to another. *Stretching* is a good word for it."

Tension is another term to describe the growth process and the positive outcomes of stretching across the quadrants. Tension can be thought of as both the act of stretching between points and a state of unease that is produced by stretching. Working through tension can be a powerful, productive experience. Michelle's tears in response to the student survey marked a turning point. She knew that her relationships with students—and, ultimately, student outcomes—would not improve unless she worked through her discomfort. According to one teacher, "This [process] is good for getting you out of your rut. You get into comfort zones and unless someone forces you to come out of them, you stay. So this is good. You need someone to say, 'You need to look at those uncomfortable areas' because, if not, they stay uncomfortable for a very long time."

This quote is especially meaningful in terms of our tendency to build up immunities to change, as discussed in chapter 3. We are exceptionally good at coping with minor discomforts because of the fears associated with deep change. To produce deep change, the tension must be surfaced and engaged in meaningful ways. Many of the tools developed to support this work help teachers expose and examine tensions in their practice.

The other meaning of *tension* is a state of unease or discomfort. Many of the teachers who participated in the pilot reported that their journey was sometimes uncomfortable, but most acknowledged this as a necessary part of the process. The following quotes speak to this dynamic:

- ◼ "My best gauge [of progress] might be my level of anxiety when looking at things."

- ◼ "You know you're doing it right if it feels difficult. That's when real reflection happens."

- ◼ "If you feel like you are doing something different for you, and you're uncomfortable with what you're doing, that means you're doing it correctly because you're stretching yourself."

Often when we try something new, things get worse before they get better, so one of our biggest challenges was helping teachers work through their discomfort. We encouraged teachers to identify small changes that they could begin implementing in their classrooms. These small experiments allowed teachers to safely fail and learn their way into more-effective ways of being with their students.

Key Processes and Supports for Professional Learning

Over the past two years, we have had the opportunity to study and learn from more than 50 teachers who participated in two separate pilot programs. Participants ranged from kindergarten to high school teachers in the four core subject areas: math, English language arts, science, and social studies. We return to Stephanie's experiences in the pilot to high-light some of the key components of this approach.

Self-Paced, Self-Directed Learning

Stephanie felt empowered by her experiences in the pilot program. Teachers begin this process by completing a series of three online courses that introduce the Connect Framework. The Reflect Assessment, which enables teachers to assess their practice relative to the quadrants of the framework, is embedded in these online courses. Stephanie's assessment results showed that her overall strengths were in the green and yellow quadrants while her primary area of growth was in the blue quadrant.

The online courses prepared Stephanie and the other the members of her PLT to use the framework to engage in deeper conversations about effective practice and their professional growth. Meeting agendas helped move teachers from discussions about strengths and weaknesses to conversations about the design and the implementation of a professional growth plan. Stephanie appreciated the opportunity to take a lot of time to identify an area of focus for her growth plan because the plan became very personal.

Through personal reflection, conversations with her PLT, and examining other sources of data about her teaching practice, Stephanie decided that her stretch into the blue quadrant would focus on raising the achievement of students who were reading below grade level. She also wanted to increase expectations for all of her students. Stephanie's school did not have designated intervention time built into the schedule, but she realized that she had to create this time for her students: "I always used to work at random, doing a little of this and a little of that. I wanted to help my students, but the timing was always a factor. I wasn't sure how to meet the needs of all my students with so little time in the day. Once I examined my data, I knew there were five students who needed the most intervention."

Although the red quadrant was not one of her highest areas overall, the Reflect Assessment also helped Stephanie recognize that she had a particular strength within the red quadrant: developing consistent routines. She created an intervention plan and established a new classroom routine that included daily, small-group instruction time for students who needed additional help. Her first step was to train her students on how to work within a group so she could implement literature circles: "Once you prepare the students and set them off on their own, they're fine....You've got to put in the time to get those students to the point where they know what to do every day; otherwise you would just have students kind of going off and doing their own thing."

While her gifted cluster worked independently, Stephanie was able to work with those students who needed additional help. After meeting consistently with her intervention students for several weeks, Stephanie saw growth in both their test scores and their confidence.

The Power of Collaboration

The concept of PLTs and teacher-based teams is not new, but working with a peer group to focus on professional practice is a new experience for many educators. One participant in the pilot program told us, "One of the main things that I've told my team about this PLT is that it has opened my eyes to what a PLT should be. Before in our PLT meetings, we have gotten together to talk about maintenance items such as field trips, what student isn't doing work, etc. I've explained that the PLT is there to challenge each other and to share and collaborate about practices that work in our class."

Nearly all teachers identified the opportunity to work with colleagues as a high point of this process. Working with colleagues provided a safe space to explore practice. PLT members were springboards and idea-generators, and they helped motivate, sustain, and encourage one another. Well-functioning peer groups provide both support (yellow quadrant) and accountability (blue quadrant). Stephanie talked to us about these aspects of her PLT: "The accountability factor was there, and I needed that. There are so many professional development opportunities over the years that I've enjoyed and feel were beneficial, but I didn't always implement them in my daily routine/classroom procedures because I already had so much going on. Plus, who was there to make sure I actually did it? With [this process] I checked in with my colleagues each week....They listened, provided feedback, and supported me. I could do the same for them."

Peer support also became critical when PLT members felt stuck or uncertain about how to proceed with their growth plan. For example, one teacher reported, "More than anything, what was helpful was simply hearing that the small progress I am making is still progress. My team is very supportive in this struggle, and their encouragement is key right now in motivating me to continue in this process."

Another teacher reported that she was struggling with the scope and the direction of her project and in danger of staying within her comfort zone. A colleague provided the straightforward push in the precise direction she needed to go to stretch her practice. She attributes her progress to both the support of her PLT and the push from her colleague: "There is nothing like having an associate in your corner. This group with whom I am working has pushed me in the green area—naturally—just by setting high expectations." In sum, for many of the teacher participants, working within a supportive yet challenging group of peers was a major highlight of the pilot program, and it helped teachers become more focused in the ways they examined and expanded their professional practice.

It was also the case that working through the growth plans affected the strength and the quality of the PLT. One teacher reported, "Our conversations have gotten better."

Another teacher recounted, "We're learning how to challenge each other and work with each other and improve each other." Stephanie already had good relationships with her colleagues, but the PLT brought them closer. Another member of Stephanie's PLT described the impact this closeness had on their conversations: "We had deep discussions about our practice with no judgments. We all listened to each other, provided feedback, and were able to draw on each other's strengths to guide us through this powerful process."

For many teachers reflection combined with collaborative conversations were intricately connected and helped push their learning forward. Professional collaboration is a tool that needs to be regularly exercised for it to be effective.

Within high-functioning groups, like Stephanie's PLT, teachers created environments with high levels of trust and a feeling that *I can be myself.* These comments suggest that teachers in these groups were able to engage the same kind of authentic conversations that HETs strive to bring about in their classrooms. Why is this important? As we described in chapter 6, authentic conversations stimulate a deeper level of reflection. When feedback is offered out of genuine caring rather than judgment, we are more open to receiving and acting on it. It creates a culture of inquiry, and the conversations can become transformative.

Several factors appear to contribute to higher levels of group performance. The first was having a clear, shared purpose for their work together as a PLT. Groups used meeting agendas and discussion questions as a starting point to keep their time together focused and on task. The second factor was a dedicated, weekly meeting time. A few PLTs already had collaboration time built into their school day, but most groups—including Stephanie's—had to find time to meet before or after school. Partly because of this extra logistical concern, the ideal group size appears to be three to five members. Groups with more than five members struggled to find common meeting times. None of the groups with more than five members stayed together through the end of the school year. Groups of two do not provide enough diversity of ideas, and participants struggled to move past roadblocks in the execution of their growth plans.

Participation in the PLT pilot programs was completely voluntary, which may also have affected the group dynamics. If participation were required, PLT members might feel less autonomy. We recommend starting small with a "coalition of the willing." After the initial groups are able to experience success and share their results with their peers, then begin to expand the scope of the work. The final factor that contributed to positive performance was the creation of a "lead learner" role.

Lead Learners

Engaging in authentic conversations about practice involves revealing weaknesses, shortcomings, and failures in addition to sharing strengths and successes. When done well, stretching your practice feels risky and at times uncomfortable. In short, this process hinges on a willingness to be vulnerable. Exposing both the effective and less effective aspects of practice to closer examination can lead to the discovery of unrealized capacities.

This level of trust and openness does not come naturally. We wanted to designate at least one member of each PLT as a model for this kind of learning. His or her role is not to be the leader of the group so much as to be out in front of the group as the first person to share experiences, take risks, and express vulnerability. Think back to Sarah's comments from chapter 4: "You can get kids to take risks if you can create that community, [but] you have to do it first." For others in the group to be willing to express their authentic voice, we needed someone within the group to lead by expressing his or her own authentic voice. We call this person within the group the *lead learner.*

To prepare teachers to fulfill the role of lead learner, we required them to attend a day of training. In addition to providing an overview of the process, resources, and expectations, the training gives lead learners an opportunity to practice engaging in more authentic conversations.

This approach to professional learning centers on teachers learning from teachers—sharing best practices, engaging in productive dialogue, and implementing change in a supportive environment. As one teacher explained, "Mutual experimentation helped us take risks. I felt more willing to share because I saw [my colleagues] willing to go there." Lead learners play a critical role in creating a productive community for learning.

Triggering Growth

Over the course of the pilot program, we documented the participants' experiences by collecting written reflections and growth plans. We conducted check-in meetings, focus groups, and interviews to gain deeper insight into the process and the impact it had on teachers. Many teachers, like Stephanie, described incremental changes in their teaching practice. They broadened and deepened their skills in a particular aspect of their practice. Some teachers, like Michelle, also experienced deep change. Participating in the pilot profoundly shifted the way they thought about themselves, their students, and their teaching practice. Both types of change led to positive outcomes in the classroom. We use stories shared by our pilot participants to illustrate the triggers that led to these two types of change. If we can better understand how these teachers grew and developed, it may be possible to jump-start the improvement process for ourselves and for others.

Incremental Change

Incremental change unfolds as we experiment with new techniques and develop new knowledge and capabilities. This kind of growth can be thought of as adding tools to the toolbox rather than redesigning or rethinking the toolbox. In many ways the change we are talking about is reflected in the attributes of the green quadrant of the Connect Framework. It is about continuously adapting, learning from what happens in the moment, and adding new skills to fill out one's practice. Teachers talked primarily about two ways that the Connect process facilitated this type of growth. First, the framework gave them a set of categories that they could use to evaluate their practice as a whole. Second, developing and implementing a personalized growth plan helped teachers address persistent sources of frustration in their practice.

Evaluating Current Practice

The Connect Framework and related resources provide a common experience, tools, and language to more easily explore the complexities of teaching and what it means to grow one's practice. One teacher reported,

"Reexamining many of the practices that I thought worked has helped me to become a better teacher."

According to another teacher, "I appreciate the four quadrants as a way to focus my attention; instead of just saying to myself, *How did today go?* I can be more specific. I am going to continue to reference those quadrants and use them to reflect on my teaching. It is a focused yet quick way to evaluate myself on a daily basis."

As teachers worked on their growth plans, they gained a greater understanding of the intersection of the practices within the four quadrants and an appreciation for the importance of balance: "It allowed me to view my teaching overall. I think had I not been challenged by the quadrants and by what the quadrants told me based upon taking the assessment, I probably would not be taking the steps to make the growth that I feel like I've made in my classroom. It's benefited me, but more than anything I feel like it's benefited my students. And I feel like I have created a better learning environment for them."

This approach to professional learning enables teachers to view their practice as a whole and then use the quadrants to home in on the specific aspects of their practice that need additional attention. Several teachers remarked that their experiences in the pilot program transformed the way they engage in reflection about their practice. They realized that their previous reflections tended to be "more general" and focus solely on external factors such as the content, the lesson, or the students. Participating in the pilot redirected their gaze inward as they considered their role in creating the learning environment. One teacher commented, "I had an 'aha' around how powerful reflection is, really true, deep reflection—not just about a lesson, or how a test could be better, but about our practice,…about our teaching as a whole. We get so consumed by the day to day;…without this opportunity I don't know that we would really look at our teaching as a whole. This pointed out things that would have been on the back burner otherwise."

It is difficult to grow without reflection. Yet it is also difficult to step back from the myriad demands of the school day to explore patterns and to critically examine what is working and what is not working. Teachers always need extra time to provide additional assistance to students, to fill out forms, to collect different kinds of student performance data, and to plan lessons for learners at different stages of understanding. The routine, daily demands of teaching are constant. Yet focused reflection has an impact on classroom practices as is evident by this teacher's feedback about the pilot program: "This project forced me to reflect on a more daily basis than I typically do, which, in turn, helped my teaching immediately. I would consistently think: *Am I hitting all the areas (red, yellow, green, and blue) with this lesson or activity? Does this lesson revert back to my comfort zone, or am I making sure to keep things balanced? What can I do for this class to help in the red but still push the blue and green?*"

In addition to providing a collaborative, supportive structure for teachers to reflect on their teaching practice in a more focused manner, this approach helps teachers recognize when they were beginning to slip back into old habits. One teacher commented, "It takes a good deal of focused thought and effort to push yourself outside your day-to-day comfort zone of what works in your classroom." The same teacher noted that the Connect Framework allowed him to "challenge myself and work outside of what I knew to work for me." The framework becomes a tool for improvement when it is used to continuously monitor and assess practice across the four dimensions of effective practice.

Similarly, the framework helps teachers who are early in their careers home in on an area of their practice that needed closer attention. Even the best pre-service teacher education programs do not fully prepare you to make the transition from student to professional. Not surprisingly, many beginning teachers need to focus on developing foundational elements of good teaching practice before they can work to stretch and connect those elements to create more powerful teaching practices. As we explored in chapters 3 and 4, often the greatest need for new teachers is to develop red and yellow quadrant skills such as classroom management, planning, and building positive working relationships with students.

One first-year teacher in our pilot was not surprised to see that her greatest area of need was in the red quadrant. She was not only new to the classroom but also assigned to teach a subject area that was outside her comfort zone. In reflecting on her challenges in the red quadrant, she found that most of her issues stemmed from poor planning. She also realized that she needed to develop structures and processes to help her more effectively follow her plan for each class period. Initially, she relied on a mental checklist, but this was insufficient. Without a set daily agenda, a lot of class time was wasted on transitions. It was also easier to get off task when she did not have a visual reminder of what she wanted to accomplish each day. Her growth plan helped her find ways to use her class time more efficiently, and it also reduced the stress she felt while planning and teaching.

Addressing Frustrations

Many teachers used their growth plan to systematically target a long-standing area of dissatisfaction in their practice. For Katrina, "point grubbing" was a constant source of frustration. She wanted her students to stop fixating on their grade: "My focus has always been on the students, their learning....Can they take targets that they've missed or they have yet to master and continue to work on that information?...This entire process has been getting the kids to do that, and providing the opportunities for them to see the value in mastering the targets—not just looking at a quiz and saying, 'Oh, I got a B. That's good enough for me. Let's move on.'"

Katrina wanted her students to take more ownership and use their assessment results to guide their learning. Another member of her PLT was focusing on a similar issue. As her colleague described what she was doing to engage students in reflection about their own learning, Katrina realized that if she "tweaked" the process it would also work with her students. She needed to do more to prompt her students to think about their learning in terms of mastery instead of as a score written on their paper. Building on her strengths in the blue and red quadrants, she created a worksheet to help students track their own progress. She described the change that the worksheet had on her students' perceptions of assessments: "Instead of students merely looking at a quiz score as a means of determining success, they now view the quiz along with their targets sheets to determine what targets have been mastered or not. This way students are better able to gauge where they are in the learning process before taking a unit assessment."

This information enabled her to provide additional learning opportunities, aligned with the targets that students still needed to master. Katrina also found that she needed to "relinquish some control" (red quadrant) in her interactions with students to encourage them to take more ownership of their learning. For example, instead of responding to students' questions with an answer, she began to help them figure out how to answer their own questions.

As she implemented these changes in her classroom, students' behavior began to change. Katrina noted, "The greatest benefit from this process has been the meaningful conversations that have taken place as a result of the project implementation....I have been answering more questions about how to master targets instead of answering questions on how to get more points." She noticed that students were "willing to go further and seek out additional assistance to master the material." Her students also shared that they felt better prepared to study for exams because they knew where they needed to focus their efforts. Katrina, like the HETs introduced earlier, wanted to transform her students into lifelong learners. She felt stuck and frustrated. As she examined this issue in collaboration with her peers through the lens of the four quadrants, Katrina found ways to attract her students toward a new way of thinking about their learning.

Deep Change

Deep change or transformative learning involves a fundamental shift in perspective as assumptions are challenged and ultimately altered. When we experience something novel or unexpected, it can open our minds and hearts to a new and more inclusive way of seeing. When this happens we begin to reconstruct how we make sense of and act on the world around us. Connect facilitates the process of deep change by enabling participants to focus on their professional practice in a qualitatively different way. Many teachers reported that collaborating with colleagues as they developed their growth plan gave them the opportunity to confront, explore, and question some of their most basic assumptions about teaching and learning.

Reframing Strengths, Weaknesses, and Growth

The Connect Framework provided teachers with a new way to think about strengths, weaknesses, and growth. For example, one teacher noted that as she stretched into the red quadrant to develop more organized processes for reviewing, assessing, and keeping track of her lesson planning, her definitions of organization and structure shifted radically: "I used to think too much organization was stifling; now I think that organization can help me be free."

Another teacher described the dramatic transformation in her perceived ability to grow as a professional:

> I used to think about the four quadrants as separate domains—and, worse, things someone was either naturally good at or not….I lived in the yellow [quadrant] and was proud of it. I always just let the other domains fall into place, never really thinking that I could "help" my natural inclinations to either grow…or decline! Thinking about them in tension with each other—related to each other, both positively and negatively—stretched my perception not only about the domains explicitly but about the concept of growth more significantly. I have never been one to merely pull folders out of a cabinet and do the same thing year after year. Being okay with that amount of change in lesson planning seemed significant enough, but this is a paradigm shift. That I don't have to flounder in my weaknesses any more—that if afforded the time…and the articulation of the weakness that real results could ensue.

Michelle's story at the beginning of this chapter is also an example of deep change. Prior to engaging in this work, she believed that her role "as a stern, strict, rigorous instructor was the only thing that mattered." Her stance was *I don't care if they like me; I want them to respect me.* Discussing the results of the Reflect Assessment forced her to reexamine how she viewed the relational dimension (yellow quadrant) of her practice. As she experimented with improving her rapport with students, her assumptions about the value of relationships in her classroom were challenged. The experience left her with a more expansive view of her practice in which the blue and yellow quadrants were no longer in constant tension:

What I have learned, and what I *now* think, is that the two are not mutually exclusive. I can be strict, stern, and rigorous (and fair) *and* have a good, solid rapport with my students. I also used to think that students really don't deserve to argue with me about grades (like on subjective interpretive material), but I *now* think that I am not perfect and some assignment evaluations deserve discussion. Both of these realizations have helped me look at my students more often as intelligent, sentient beings—not as empty vessels waiting to be filled by all I have to offer.

Michelle's expanded view of teaching makes room for both the directive and the co-creative perspectives. Michelle also gained one more critical insight into her teaching practice: The reflective process helped her turn her gaze inward. She began to see that the ongoing tension she was experiencing with some of her students was not just a problem located within her students. She was part of the problem. Rather than trying to more tightly control her students' behavior (red quadrant), she realized that she needed to "loosen her grip on students a little bit" and more closely regulate her own behavior. She reflected on the shift in her perspective: "I used to think that kids didn't like me as a teacher because I was rigorous, but I now know that some students felt like I didn't like them, that I thought they were stupid, that I just have a cold personality."

Once Michelle redefined the problem as something that she was contributing to, she could make changes in her own behavior.

Confronting Fears

Deep change almost always involves confronting a fear or a deeply held assumption about teaching or learning. We expect change to be associated with uncertainty and ambiguity, but the kind of fear that we are referring to is far more insidious and deeply buried because it requires us to confront our underlying[5] or hidden assumptions.[6] These beliefs are so ingrained that they become part of our "truth." They are assumed to be fact and are rarely tested. In challenging these fears and assumptions, we are, in essence, challenging our own identity. We cannot emerge from this process as the same person.

Michelle's identity as a teacher was wrapped up in her assumptions about control. She took pride in her reputation as being challenging and strict. Students knew not to act up in her class, and she did not want to compromise on her high expectations for performance and behavior: "I didn't want to be that [yellow quadrant] teacher. I'm not their buddy, and I think, in my resistance to that, I went to the other end of the spectrum." By allowing herself to stretch into the yellow quadrant, she learned that her fears were unfounded: "What this whole thing has…revealed to me is that it doesn't have to be this intimidation kind of factor." She could still hold high standards for her students and have a well-behaved class while working to improve her rapport with them. At the end of the pilot program, Michelle discovered that the only thing she had lost was "this prefixed vision of myself that was like rock-hard."

Jodi is another teacher who confronted a fear closely tied to her identity as a teacher. Unlike Michelle, who struggled to connect the blue and yellow quadrants, Jodi found it natural to connect the two. She is able to get her students to work hard and achieve at a high level because of her rapport with them. At her school Jodi has a reputation for "being a teacher that students want to have because they like me," and that reputation is very important to her.

One of Jodi's growth areas was in the red quadrant. In particular she struggled with how strict to be and how much to enforce school and class rules because she worried that it would have a negative impact on her relationship with students. As a result of thinking about her teaching practice relative to the four quadrants, she began to notice that the students in one of her classes were taking advantage her reputation of being "the nice teacher." During class they regularly used their cell phones to send text messages. Jodi decided to take a stand. She made the students turn off their cell phones and place them on top of their desks that so she could see them. She told herself, *I'm weak in this area, and I need to get better at it, and I'm just going to enforce this rule.* The results of this experiment surprised her: "[The students] responded really well to that. Rather than, I guess I always thought, *Oh, the students won't like me if I'm strict and I enforce the rules.* Instead they responded very positively and seemed to appreciate that I was enforcing the rules because they could see that by not doing it, it was impeding their learning."

Even on days when Jodi forgot to remind students about the new rule, they continued to follow it. The experience taught her that she did not have to give up or compromise on the yellow quadrant to become stronger in the red quadrant: "I am now more aware of my teaching in terms of the quadrants, and I have been paying more attention to whether or not I am neglecting certain quadrants. I have come to realize that there should be more of a balance between my desire to have a good rapport with my students and my need to establish more control in the classroom."

This process provides an opportunity for teachers not only to reflect on practice but also to explore and test individual assumptions about the nature of teaching and learning.

Summary

Through the use of the Connect Framework, teachers feel a renewed appreciation for the role of balance, negotiating tensions, and stretching their practice. This approach enables teachers to explore their classroom practice in ways that lead to deeper reflection, more focused conversations and collaboration, and more systematic efforts to improve effectiveness. The framework gives teachers a common language of practice that they can use to question assumptions about teaching and learning. Like the epigraph by Kahn, the framework provides "a perspective that allows us a fresh look at our most basic assumptions about teaching and learning." As participants in the pilot program engaged in an iterative process of reflection, discussion, and action, they noticed positive student outcomes.

🌰 *PLANTING SEEDS*

1. Before she started the pilot program, Michelle believed that rapport with students was overrated. She liked being perceived as rigorous, stern, and strict. In what ways does your own perception of yourself limit your capacity to maximize students' academic growth?

2. To assess her practice at a deeper level, Michelle surveyed her students about the qualities that they desire in a teacher. When she examined the results, she found that her teaching did not align very well with these descriptions. This was a key factor in Michelle's choice to work on the yellow aspects of her practice. When have you used your students to help you assess your practice? What did you learn about yourself?

3. Michelle assumed that she would lose her reputation as a rigorous teacher if she spent more time and effort working in the yellow quadrant. What assumptions do you have about what would happen if you spent more time and effort working in your growth quadrant?

GROWING YOUR PRACTICE

1. When you consider your practice relative to the Connect Framework, what is your primary area of strength? How is this strength reflected in your day-to-day practice? Identify one way that you can leverage your strengths to stretch your practice. Use the stories in this chapter as examples.

2. When you consider your practice relative to the framework, what is your primary area of growth? What might your practice be like if you were able to act out of the attributes associated with this quadrant on a more regular basis? Identify one skill or practice associated with your growth quadrant that you can work on to increase your capacity in that quadrant.

3. With whom could you create a PLT? Write down the names of two or three people whom you could invite to be part of a PLT.

Strategies for Moving Forward

Education is not the filling of a pail, but the lighting of a fire.

— Anonymous

THIS BOOK IS AN INVITATION TO BECOME THE BEST TEACHER IN YOU again and again.

As you continue to reflect on what you have read, you have the opportunity to open new paths to your own development. To help clinch the learning, let's quickly review the key storyline of the book.

In chapter 1 you were introduced to Kelli's story and to two overarching perspectives associated with teaching and learning: the directive and co-creative perspectives. These are not black-and-white, either/or choices. The co-creative perspective grows out of the directive perspective but asks more of us, as it includes students as real partners in the teaching/learning process. Said another way, the co-creative perspective transcends but includes the directive perspective. In Kelli's story we see how a pivotal moment in your teaching experience can help you move toward the co-creative perspective.

In chapter 2 we introduce the Connect Framework, which further differentiates the directive and co-creative perspectives into four distinct quadrants of effective teaching. Each of the quadrants represents a different orientation toward effective practice:

- **Yellow quadrant** Relationships: cultivating a supportive community

- **Green quadrant** Continuous improvement: adapting and embracing change

■ **Blue quadrant**   High expectations: maximizing every
                       student's achievement

■ **Red quadrant**   Stable environment: creating structures
                       and processes

We introduce the notion of powerful practice, a behavior or set of behaviors that crosses the boundaries of the framework and links the quadrants in mutually reinforcing ways. Diana's story provides an initial illustration of the powerful practices that emerge as teachers learn to integrate the quadrants.

Chapters 3 and 4 focus on what it means to stretch your practice across the four quadrants. Most of us have a natural affinity for one of the quadrants. This quadrant is like your home; it is the dimension that feels the most comfortable to you. In chapter 3 we describe Aaron's stretch out of the red quadrant, and in chapter 4 we describe Sarah's stretch into the yellow quadrant. A fruitful path for development is to leverage an area of strength to become more conversant in an area that feels less comfortable. In many cases this means developing new skills, but it also may involve opening the mind and the heart to ideas that currently feel paradoxical. For this reason it often takes difficult circumstances to trigger movement toward this kind of deep change.

In chapters 5 and 6, we talk about higher-level capacities that emerge as we begin to integrate all four quadrants. In chapter 5 we use Laurie's story to explore one of these higher-level capacities: self-empowerment. Self-empowerment emerges as teachers take full responsibility for what happens in their classrooms in the face of powerful and often conflicting external demands. We typically think about responsibilities in terms of a job description, but a job description is externally generated. When we become self-empowered, we understand and acknowledge these external demands, but we choose our stance and our course of action based on our own internal compass.

In chapter 6 we use Vicki's story to illustrate another higher-level capacity: transformational leadership in the classroom. Transformational leadership emerges as teachers take full responsibility for the outcomes in their classroom while making students partners in the enterprise at the same time. Often responsibility and control are centralized under the leader. Transformational leaders assume responsibility for outcomes, but they enact their practice through student ownership of the learning. When this capacity emerges, the teacher shifts into a facilitative role and the students become self-empowered leaders themselves. Students, even those who are normally resistant, buy into what is being asked of them, and they take leadership in moving themselves and others toward the desired outcomes. Learning is accelerated and lives change because they live in a community of transformative learning.

In chapter 7 the focus shifts away from understanding the co-creative perspective toward becoming a teacher who *lives* the co-creative perspective. Chapter 7 uses the concepts that were developed in the first six chapters to lay out a path of personal development. We use Michelle's story of transformation to outline a process of growth that is relevant to us all. This is the pivotal chapter of the book because it moves away from description and explanation toward the development of your own personal practice.

We close the book with an invitation to start your own personal journey toward the best teacher in you. We offer the following suggestions to help you begin your own journey.

- Complete the Reflect Assessment in Resource A and the Organizational Culture Assessment Instrument for Classrooms in Resource B to assess your teaching practice and the current culture of your classroom relative to the four quadrants of the Connect Framework. Which of the quadrants represents an area of strength? Which of the quadrants represents an area of growth? How can you leverage your strengths to help stretch your teaching practice into the other quadrants? Be specific.

- Form a professional learning team that will meet regularly to provide both support and accountability as you work to stretch and grow your practice. Share with your PLT colleagues the results of your assessments in the first suggestion above. Invite them to take the assessments as well. Think about how you might take advantage of the strengths and the skills that other team members possess. You may want to use the Appreciative Inquiry Protocol (Resource C) to explore one another's strengths. What insights and support can you offer one another? Discuss how you can all be helpful to one another as each of you charts your own course toward excellence. Recognize that each of you will need to find your own pathway. Your PLT will be particularly helpful when you encounter obstacles or barriers. Your teammates can help you make sense of those experiences and learn from them.

■ Identify one area of your practice that could benefit from closer attention and active experimentation. It could relate to new requirements from your principal, your district, or some other entity, but ultimately this area must relate to your own self-assessment. It should leverage an area of strength in the service of an area of need. Your area of focus might be a persistent frustration in your current teaching practice or something completely innovative that you want to examine. What skills do you need to develop or refine to explore this area of focus? How can you leverage your strengths (as identified through the Reflect Assessment) to address this area of focus?

■ Create a plan. Identify specific lessons and activities that will allow you to stretch from an area of strength to an area of growth. Be specific and start small so that you can generate some positive momentum. Experiment with small but significant changes in practice. Try on new assumptions and new strategies. Be ready for what it feels like to change. As many of our teachers have said, if it feels awkward and uncomfortable, you are probably working on the right things. Don't be afraid to tell your students and others in your support network why you are seeking to stretch in new directions so that they can help you.

■ Collect some data. Invite student and peer feedback. What is working better? What still needs to be done? What ideas can they offer to help you move forward?

■ Consider using a journal to record your observations and feelings as you experiment. This will also help you see your progress as you begin your journey. In your journal assess and reflect on your growth using the data that you have collected. What worked well? What were the roadblocks? What next steps will you take to continue to stretch your practice? Get support and advice from your colleagues and continue to move forward.

If you feel like you need more help to get started, visit the BFK•Connect website (BFKConnect.org). Here you can get information about additional blended learning offerings and other resources to support you and your team in this important work.

You can also visit the Celebrate Teaching website (Celebrate Teaching.org). View a video. Be inspired by the profiles and the stories of teachers who pursue excellence on a daily basis.

In the end excellence is its own reward. When you seriously pursue a path of improvement, you will find yourself more excited and energized by your work and more motivated to take the difficult next steps that improvement requires.

Resource A: The Reflect Assessment

NOTE THE 12 PRACTICES LISTED BELOW AND THINK ABOUT HOW THEY frame your orientation to teaching and learning in your classroom. Rank each practice based on how central that practice is to your work in the classroom. Begin by putting a 12 next to the item that is **most prominent** in your practice and a 1 next to the item that is **least prominent** in your practice. Continue until you have ranked each of the practices.

A _____ Adapting lessons in response to student cues

B _____ Empowering students

C _____ Communicating clear expectations for behavior

D _____ Cultivating creativity and spontaneity

E _____ Challenging students to do their best

F _____ Establishing a culture of accountability in the classroom

G _____ Organizing learning activities and resources

H _____ Setting clear goals and monitoring progress

I _____ Building trust

J _____ Making learning relevant to students

K _____ Facilitating teamwork and cooperation

L _____ Maximizing instruction and learning time

Reminder: 12 = most prominent, 1 = least prominent

When you have completed your rank ordering, go to the next page to score your results.

Scoring the Reflect Assessment

Score your responses to the Reflect Assessment following the criteria below. Then plot your scores on the scale in the appropriate quadrant on the next page.

Yellow Quadrant

Plot your average score for items B, I, and K on the scale in the *yellow* quadrant.

Item	Score
B	
I	
K	
Average of B, I, and K	

Green Quadrant

Plot your average score for items A, D, and J on the scale in the *green* quadrant.

Item	Score
A	
D	
J	
Average of A, D, and J	

Blue Quadrant

Plot your average score for items E, F, and H on the scale in the *blue* quadrant.

Item	Score
E	
F	
H	
Average of E, F, and H	

Red Quadrant

Plot your average score for items C, G, and L on the scale in the ***red*** quadrant.

Item	Score
C	
G	
L	
Average of C, G, and L	

Reflect Assessment Results Profile

Connect the dots to get a sense of the relative importance of the attributes that tend to drive your practice.

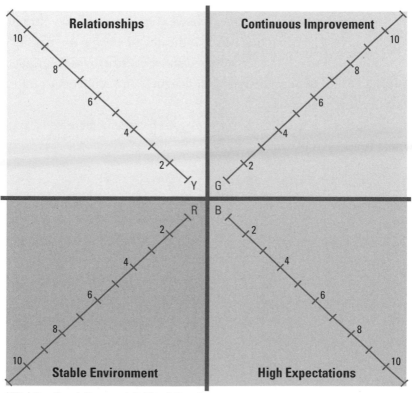

KEY | Y: yellow | G: green | B: blue | R: red

Interpreting the Results of Your Reflect Assessment

Once you have completed your results profile, the next step is to interpret the results. There are two important factors to consider when interpreting your profile.

- Note the relative magnitude of the average scores in each of the quadrants. The larger the average score, relative to the others, the more central that set of attributes is to your practice.

- Consider the relationship between the quadrants. Are you able to connect these attributes in your practice?

An average score that is greater than 6.0 indicates a high affinity to the attributes associated with that quadrant. An average score of less than 6.0 indicates a lower affinity to those attributes.

Conclusion

The results of the Reflect Assessment enable you to assess the key attributes in your current teaching practice. It indicates *where you are right now.*

Your next step is to assess *where you would like to be.* Continue to reflect and talk to administrators, colleagues, and students to inform your development goals.

Your final step will be to *close the gaps* between where you are and where you would like to be.

Resource B: Organizational Culture Assessment Instrument for Classrooms

T HE PURPOSE OF THE ORGANIZATIONAL CULTURE ASSESSMENT Instrument for Classrooms[1] (OCAI-C) is to assess six key dimensions of classroom culture. In completing the instrument, you will be providing a picture of the fundamental assumptions on which your classroom operates and the attributes that characterize your classroom culture. There are no right or wrong answers. Every classroom will most likely be described by a different set of responses. Therefore be as accurate as you can in responding to the items so that your resulting cultural diagnosis will be as precise as possible.

The OCAI-C consists of six items. Each item has four alternatives. Divide 100 points among these four alternatives, depending on the extent to which each alternative is similar to your classroom. Give a higher number of points to the alternative that is most similar to your classroom. For example, on item 1, if you think alternative A is very similar to your classroom, alternatives B and C are somewhat similar, and alternative D is hardly similar at all, you might give 55 points to A, 20 points each to B and C, and 5 points to D. You may use any combination of points; just be sure that your total equals 100 for each item.

Note that the response column on the left is labeled "Now." These responses mean that you are rating your classroom culture as it is *currently*. Complete that rating first.

When you have finished, imagine your classroom culture as you think it *should be for students to flourish and exceed expectations*. Complete the instrument again, this time responding to the items as if your classroom culture has produced extraordinary success. Write these responses in the "Preferred" column. Your responses will produce two independent ratings of your culture—one as it currently exists and one as you wish it to be for students to flourish and exceed expectations.

When you have completed each of the six items, for both the current culture and the preferred culture, use the scoring sheet to tally your responses. Then use the scoring graphic to map your responses.

The Organizational Culture Assessment Instrument for Classrooms

1. Dominant Characteristics	*Now*	*Preferred*
A. My classroom is a student-centered place. Students feel like they belong to an extended family; they seem to share a lot of themselves.		
B. My classroom is an innovative, lively, and enthusiastic place. Students are excited and willing to take risks in order to learn.		
C. My classroom is a results-oriented place. The concern is with the accomplishment of objectives and maximizing learning. Students are industrious and achievement oriented.		
D. My classroom is an orderly and structured place. Students feel secure and are willing to follow the rules.		
Total	100	100

2. Teacher Attention

	Now	*Preferred*
A. As a teacher, my attention is generally focused on mentoring, facilitating, and supporting students.		
B. As a teacher, my attention is generally focused on engaging students in creative learning.		
C. As a teacher, my attention is generally focused on setting high expectations and establishing a sense of urgency for learning.		
D. As a teacher, my attention is generally focused on managing, organizing, and working efficiently.		
Total	100	100

3. Classroom Management

	Now	*Preferred*
A. My classroom management style gives rise to student involvement, participation, and collaboration.		
B. My classroom management style gives rise to student autonomy, experimentation, and creativity.		
C. My classroom management style gives rise to student determination, industriousness, and extra effort.		
D. My classroom management style gives rise to a sense of student security, predictability, and stability.		
Total	100	100

4. Classroom Glue

	Now	*Preferred*
A. The glue that holds my classroom together is mutual respect, trust, and loyalty. The students believe in and support one another.		
B. The glue that holds my classroom together is vision, optimism, and hope. The students believe in their ability to improvise and adapt.		
C. The glue that holds my classroom together is individual goal accomplishment. The students see that they are achieving goals and believe that they can succeed.		
D. The glue that holds my classroom together is expectations and routines. The students believe that what is supposed to happen will happen.		
Total	100	100

5. Strategic Emphasis

	Now	*Preferred*
A. My strategy is to promote collaboration. Learning accelerates because of caring, openness, and mutual trust.		
B. My strategy is to engage students' imaginations. Learning is accelerated through relevant experiences, creative engagement, and inspiring discoveries.		
C. My strategy is to promote individual success. Learning is accelerated through stretch targets and personal accountability.		
D. My strategy is to promote a sense of personal security, safety, and stability. Learning is accelerated because the work is predictable and unfolds as expected.		
Total	100	100

6. Criteria of Success

	Now	Preferred
A. My classroom is successful when we enrich our person-to-person connections. My students leave with the capacity to respect, listen, and learn from peers.		
B. My classroom is successful when we are able to envision and pursue possibilities. My students leave with the capacity to adapt, invent, and originate.		
C. My classroom is successful when we focus on goals and set high expectations for the quality of work. My students leave with the capacity to set goals, persevere, and achieve.		
D. My classroom is successful when we have established clear structures and routines. My students leave with the capacity to self-monitor, follow directions, and be good citizens.		
Total	100	100

Worksheet for Scoring the OCAI-C

Now Scores		*Preferred* Scores
	1A	1A

Now Scores

	1A
	2A
	3A
	4A
	5A
	6A
	Sum (total of A responses)
	Average (sum divided by 6)

	1B
	2B
	3B
	4B
	5B
	6B
	Sum (total of B responses)
	Average (sum divided by 6)

	1C
	2C
	3C
	4C
	5C
	6C
	Sum (total of C responses)
	Average (sum divided by 6)

	1D
	2D
	3D
	4D
	5D
	6D
	Sum (total of D responses)
	Average (sum divided by 6)

Preferred Scores

	1A
	2A
	3A
	4A
	5A
	6A
	Sum (total of A responses)
	Average (sum divided by 6)

	1B
	2B
	3B
	4B
	5B
	6B
	Sum (total of B responses)
	Average (sum divided by 6)

	1C
	2C
	3C
	4C
	5C
	6C
	Sum (total of C responses)
	Average (sum divided by 6)

	1D
	2D
	3D
	4D
	5D
	6D
	Sum (total of D responses)
	Average (sum divided by 6)

Using *black* ink:

1. Plot the average of your A scores in the *yellow* quadrant.

2. Plot the average of your B scores in the *green* quadrant.

3. Plot the average of your C scores in the *blue* quadrant.

4. Plot the average of your D scores in the *red* quadrant.

5. Connect the dots.

Using *blue* ink:

1. Plot the average of your A scores in the *yellow* quadrant.

2. Plot the average of your B scores in the *green* quadrant.

3. Plot the average of your C scores in the *blue* quadrant.

4. Plot the average of your D scores in the *red* quadrant.

5. Connect the dots.

Scoring Graphic for the OCAI-C

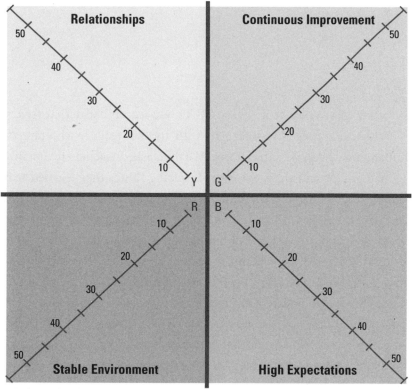

KEY | Y: yellow | G: green | B: blue | R: red

Resource C: Appreciative Inquiry Protocol

I N OUR EARLY WORKSHOPS WITH HETs, WE ASKED EACH TEACHER TO conduct an appreciative interview with another teacher who taught a similar grade level and subject area. We then asked teachers to assemble in small groups and share the most inspiring things they learned from their partner. As teachers shared what they had learned, we began to hear the themes that ground this book. Appreciative inquiry is a great tool for research and professional development. It allows you to focus attention on the positive aspects of the current situation rather than just on what is broken. It also allows you to reflect on what is good and should be preserved as you move forward toward excellence. Below you see the appreciative inquiry protocol that was used over the first two years of this project. You may want to partner with a colleague and use this protocol to explore the strengths in each other's practice.

1. Think back over your entire career as a teacher—from your earliest memories to today. Now think about a peak experience or a high point, a time when you experienced yourself as most *effective* and most *satisfied* as a teacher.

   ■ What sets this experience apart?

   ■ What contextual factors (e.g., room arrangement, curricular materials, choice of content) contributed to your high level of effectiveness and satisfaction?

   ■ What made this a good lesson for your students?

   ■ What gets in the way of having this kind of experience every day?

2. Without being humble, what do you value most about:

   ■ Your approach to teaching your subject area?

■ Your ability to motivate students to enjoy your subject area?

3. What do you do to be effective with:

   ■ Low-achieving students?

   ■ High-achieving students?

   ■ Average-achieving students?

4. Fast-forward. It is five years from today, and you are beginning a new job in your district. You are responsible for helping both beginning and veteran teachers become more effective teachers. You feel more energized, confident, and successful as a teacher than at any time in the past.

   ■ What are the most important principles of practice you want to convey to these teachers?

   ■ What kinds of experiences do you provide for these teachers?

   ■ What do you tell these teachers to avoid in their practice?

   ■ What kinds of district and building support are necessary for these teachers to be as effective as you are?

Resource D: Interview Protocol

A S PART OF OUR RESEARCH FOR THIS BOOK, WE CONDUCTED THREE rounds of in-depth interview with 30 of the highest-performing teachers in the state of Ohio. For each round, we used a semistructured interview format. In other words, we created an interview guide with the key questions that we wanted to ask, but we allowed the interviews to flow like a conversation. When an interviewee made an intriguing point or shared a powerful story, we followed up with additional questions rather than use the interview guide as a formal script. In this section we share the interview guides from each round of interviews.

Round I Guide for HET Interviews (October 2010)

1. Please tell us who you are and give us a two-minute history of your career.

2. What do you most love about being a teacher?
   - What are you like when you are at your very best?
   - What for you is the essence of excellent teaching?
   - What do you find most challenging about being a teacher?

3. What is unique about your school context?

4. Over time a teacher can move from novice to master.
   - How are you different now from when you first started?
   - What events most altered your outlook?
   - What does it mean to be a master teacher?
   - What does mastery have to do with value-added scores?

5. Every class has a unique culture.
   - Describe the ideal class culture.

- At the start of school, what do you do to establish a class culture?

- How do you change as the year goes on?

- What is the culture like at the end of the year?

6. What is unique about you as a teacher?

   - What do you most value?

   - How do you stay energized?

   - What personal disciplines make you different?

7. In terms of practices, what is the most unusual or creative thing you do in each of the following areas?

   - To have an, orderly, organized, predictable class

   - To help students achieve and excel academically

   - To create a climate of collaboration and teamwork

   - To stimulate growth, development, and creativity

Round II Guide for HET Interviews (August 2011)

1. Please tell us who you are and give us a two-minute history of your career.

2. What do you most love about teaching?

3. What is it like when you are at your best?

4. What differentiates you from a teacher with average value-added scores?

5. Here is a statement about the needs and the interests of students. What does this statement mean to you?

   "You first learn that every kid has different needs and interests. So you work with them. Then you learn that they are actually all the same. They have a common set of needs. You develop a universal model. Then you can reach them all. Once you discover this, you can successfully teach anybody, anywhere. You will always succeed."

6. Here are some assumptions about the needs of students. Which ones are most important?

   ■ Students want to be loved and supported.

   ■ Students want to be fully challenged and engaged.

   ■ Students want to sacrifice for the good of a cohesive workgroup.

   ■ Students want to learn, grow, and successfully distinguish themselves.

   ■ Students want to see the relevance in what they are asked to do.

   ■ Students want autonomy and control over what they are asked to do.

   ■ Students want to pursue a meaningful future.

   ■ Students want predictable routines.

7. In order to excel, a teacher often has to shift from normal patterns to more unusual patterns. Listed below are some shifts teachers claim to make in relation to themselves and their students. With which of the following shifts do you identify? Which ones would you question or qualify? What other shifts would you add?

Shifts in the Teacher

   ■ *Duty to love:* "Teaching is not my job. It is my calling, my mission. Teaching makes my life meaningful."

   ■ *Information to transformation:* "I do not teach to instill knowledge; I teach to change the lives of my students. My kids do not believe that they can learn. I have to convert them."

   ■ *Secular to spiritual:* "I take home my roster and I pray over the name of each child."

   ■ *Fear to confidence:* "I ask the principal for the worst students because I know I am the only hope they have in life. I am likely the only teacher they will get who can change their lives."

   ■ *Detachment to accountability:* "If they do not learn, it is not their fault. I take accountability for each student, and I keep trying until I reach every one of them."

■ *Negative emotions to positive emotions:* "If I feel negative, I catch it and become positive. My feelings are contagious. It is my job to always be positive."

■ *External control to internal control:* "When the district mandate goes against the best interests of the kids, I change the material."

■ *Approval to independence:* "I am not worried about what they think of me. I do what I believe is right for them."

Shifts in Relating to Students

■ *Constraint to possibility:* "I see the potential in my students, and I focus them on what they can do to make a new life trajectory."

■ *Academic to relevant:* "I never teach anything unless I first make it relevant to me and then relevant to the students."

■ *Soft to challenging:* "I just push and I expect them to do the right thing, and I expect them to work hard. And when they don't, I just keep pushing."

■ *Slow to fast:* "I move quickly. We never waste a moment. Every minute matters."

■ *Boredom to engagement:* "My kids can go to the restroom anytime they want, but they never do go because they cannot stand to miss what is going on in the class."

■ *Transactional relationships to relationships of unconditional positive regard:* "If a student is disrespectful, I correct them while showing complete respect for the student."

■ *Teaching to coaching:* "I coach, encourage, and build their belief in themselves."

■ *Distrust to trust:* "My students adore me and will do anything I ask."

■ *Negative to positive peer pressure:* "The social pressure is positive. In our class we are all working for the common good. My kids walk down the hall in a different way. They willingly stay in line. There is no need for external pressure. They take personal ownership."

- *Chaos to internalized order:* "If I am not there at the start of class, my students start without me."

- *Direction to empowerment:* "I put the students in position to teach me things. I put them in positions of control: this is their class, and I expect them to teach themselves."

8. Here is a statement about instruction and facilitation. What does this statement mean to you?

"You have to stop being the center of attention. You have to move from instruction to facilitation. When you learn to facilitate, you crack the code, they learn from each other, teaching becomes easy, and they make more progress."

9. Here are some statements teachers have made when describing the conversations that take place in their class. Given your own experience, what items would you remove from the list and what items would you add?

- *Facilitation:* "I get out of the instructor role, and I start a discussion."

- *Stimulation:* "I call on the right students and in the right sequence."

- *Involvement:* "Others cannot help but piggyback on and give their opinions."

- *Focus:* "I become fully focused on the changing dynamics in the conversation."

- *Monitoring:* "I pay attention to feedback, making constant, real-time assessments."

- *Risk:* "I attempt to do new things."

- *Improvisation:* "I change on the fly, based on that group of kids, that day, that skill."

- *Outliers:* "I formulate a plan to reach the outliers. I want to involve everyone."

- *Understanding:* "The students understand the flow of where we are going."

- *Challenge:* "The task becomes an intrinsically motivating puzzle."

- *Commitment:* "Everyone is engaged, and no one is wasting time."

- *Ownership:* "Students begin to take ownership and begin to function without me."

- *Emergence:* "A dynamic web of connections emerges."

- *Seamlessness:* "They all take the right roles, and the class moves seamlessly."

- *Shared leadership:* "Initiative spontaneously moves from person to person."

- *Contagion:* "My excitement feeds back to the students and stimulates more excitement."

- *Dual focus:* "I keep the group animated while also paying attention to individuals."

- *Collective intelligence:* "The process leads to group discovery and knowledge creation."

- *Achievement:* "They are proud of what they are doing."

- *Success:* "The excitement from learning becomes self-sustaining."

- *Effortlessness:* "The process of learning and teaching becomes enjoyable and easy."

- *Love:* "They begin to love school."

- *Confidence:* "They become more confident."

- *Mutual learning:* "I am learning new things just as they are."

- *Impact:* "I feel more confident, organized, adaptive, and enthusiastic."

10. What happens when something gets in the way of learning in your classroom?

11. When did you most improve as a teacher?

12. How does your school support or discourage excellence in teaching?

Round III Guide for HET Interviews (July 2012)

1. Please tell us who you are and give us a two-minute history of your career.

2. What do you most love about being a teacher?
   - Why did you become a teacher?
   - What for you is the essence of excellent teaching?
   - What are you like when you are at your very best?

3. Over time a teacher can evolve.
   - How are you different now from when you first started?
   - What events most altered your outlook?
   - What does it mean to be a highly effective teacher?
   - What do you believe about value-added scores?

4. Some teachers feel more empowered than others. In what ways are you self-empowered?
   - What meaning do you find in teaching?
   - How autonomous are you?
   - How is your level of competence different from that of others?
   - How would you describe your relationships with students?
   - Do you believe you can reach every student?

5. Every class has a unique culture.
   - At the start of school, what do you do to establish a class culture?
   - What does who you are as a person have to do with how you teach and how your classroom operates?
   - How does the culture change as the year goes on?
   - What is the culture like at the end of the year?
   - How is your culture unique?

6. What is unique about you as a teacher?

    ■ What do you most value?

    ■ How do you stay energized?

    ■ What makes you different?

    ■ What do you find most challenging?

7. What is unique about your school context?

Resource E: Online Tools and Resources

For free downloads and information about other tools and resources related to using the BFK•Connect Framework to support professional growth, please visit BestTeacherinYou.org.

Notes

INTRODUCTION

Learning from Highly Effective Teachers

1. For more information see Raj Chetty, John N. Friedman, and Jonah E. Rockoff, "The Long-Term Impacts of Teachers: Teacher Value-Added and Student Outcomes in Adulthood" (working paper, Harvard University, 2011).

CHAPTER 1

Becoming the Best Teacher in You: A Process, Not a Destination

1. Robert E. Quinn, *Deep Change: Discovering the Leader Within* (San Francisco: Jossey-Bass, 1996). Also see Quinn's *The Deep Change Field Guide: A Personal Course to Discovering the Leader Within* (San Francisco: Jossey-Bass, 2012).

2. We value Palmer's reflections on the courage to teach. They provide us with insights on the process of becoming more effective. Parker J. Palmer, *The Courage to Teach: Exploring the Inner Landscape of a Teacher's Life* (San Francisco: Jossey-Bass, 1998), 178.

3. Albert Bandura, "Self-Efficacy: Toward a Universal Theory of Behavioral Change," *Psychological Review* 8, no. 2 (1977): 191–215.

4. Teach. In *The Free Dictionary,* accessed January 25, 2014, http://www .thefreedictionary.com/teach.

5. Robert M. Pirsig, *Zen and the Art of Motorcycle Maintenance* (New York: Morrow, 1974), 148.

6. This focus on awareness, reflection, and understanding the needs of others is consistent with notions of emotional intelligence. These ideas are further

explored in Daniel Goleman, *Emotional Intelligence* (New York: Bantam Books, 1995).

7. K. Anders Ericsson, Michael J. Prietula, and Edward T. Cokely, "The Making of an Expert," *Harvard Business Review* 85 (2007): 114–21.

CHAPTER 2

Embracing Connections: Integrating Essential Elements

1. Mike Thomas and Margie Jorgensen, *Why Are Some Teachers More Effective Than Others? The Challenges and Opportunities of Defining "Great" Teaching* (Columbus, OH: Battelle for Kids, 2010).

2. For a discussion of the interpenetration of categories, see Robert E. Quinn, Joel A. Kahn, and Michael J. Mandl, "Perspectives on Organization Change: Exploring Movement at the Interface," in *Organizational Behavior: The State of the Science*, ed. Jerald Greenberg (Hillsdale, NJ: Lawrence Erlbaum, 1995), 109–34.

3. Robert E. Quinn and John Rohrbaugh, "A Spatial Model of Effectiveness Criteria: Towards a Competing Values Approach to Organizational Analysis, *Management Science* 29, no. 3 (1983): 363–77. For a more comprehensive discussion of the competing values framework, see Kim S. Cameron, Robert E. Quinn, Jeff DeGraff, and Anjan V. Thakor, *Competing Values Leadership: Creating Value in Organizations* (North Hampton, MA: Edward Elgar, 2006). Also see Kim S. Cameron and Robert E. Quinn, *Diagnosing and Changing Organizational Culture: Based on the Competing Values Framework* (San Francisco: Jossey-Bass, 2011).

4. This is consistent with ideas of active learning, a teaching approach supported by a large body of research: John A. C. Hattie, *Visible Learning: A Synthesis of Over 800 Meta-analyses Relating to Achievement* (London: Routledge, 2009).

5. Mike Thomas and Katherine Heynoski, *Powerful Practices in the Classroom: Applying Lessons from Highly Effective Teachers to Adopt an Integrated Approach to Professional Development* (Columbus, OH: Battelle for Kids, 2013).

6. Katherine A. Lawrence, Peter Lenk, and Robert E. Quinn, "Behavioral Complexity in Leadership: The Psychometric Properties of a New Instrument

to Measure Behavioral Repertoire," *Leadership Quarterly* 20, no. 2 (2009): 87–102.

7. Robert Marzano, John Hattie, and others have found relationships between particular teacher practices and their effectiveness relative to test scores. But all of these relationships are statistical in nature. A particular practice does not guarantee success, but some practices are associated with a higher likelihood of success. See for example John Hattie, *Visible Learning for Teachers: Maximizing Impact on Learning* (London: Routledge, 2011). Also see Robert J. Marzano, Debra J. Pickering, and Jane E. Pollock, *Classroom Instruction That Works: Research-Based Strategies for Increasing Student Achievement* (Danvers, MA: McREL, 2001).

8. From the co-creative perspective, the teacher and the students are an interacting system. The teacher can use key skills to set up the enabling conditions but cannot ensure what will happen. Each interaction is unique. The overall system responds to small stimuli, and dynamics unfold in unexpected ways. Emergence is not predictable. The facilitative teacher who brings about the emergent process is constantly responding and taking action in real time. The system cannot be understood by breaking down the parts. The logic of independent and dependent variables does not hold. If learning is a complex adaptive process, traditional efforts to predict effective practices may have limited utility. For a helpful reference, see Mary Uhl-Bien, Russ Marion, and Bill McKelvey, "Complexity Leadership Theory: Shifting Leadership from the Industrial Age to the Knowledge Era," *Leadership Quarterly* 18, no. 4 (2007): 298–318.

9. C. Hampden-Turner, *Maps of the Mind: Charts and Concepts of the Mind and Its Labyrinths* (New York: Macmillan, 1982), 148.

10. For a discussion of Benedict's influence on Maslow, see Hampden-Turner, *Maps of the Mind,* 148.

11. Abraham Maslow, *Motivation and Personality* (New York: Harper and Row, 1954).

12. Mihaly Csikszentmihalyi, *Flow: The Psychology of Optimal Experience* (New York: Harper Perennial, 1990).

13. Mihaly Csikszentmihalyi, *Finding Flow: The Psychology of Engagement with Everyday Life* (New York: Basic Books, 1997), 31–32.

14. Keith Sawyer, *Group Genius: The Creative Power of Collaboration* (Philadelphia: Basic Books, 2007).

CHAPTER 3

Opening the Mind: Embracing Deep Change

1. National Commission on Teaching and America's Future, *Who Will Teach? Experience Matters* (Washington, DC: Thomas G. Carroll and Elizabeth Foster, 2010).

2. Rebecca Anhorn, "The Profession That Eats Its Young," *Delta Kappa Gamma Bulletin* 74, no. 3 (2008): 15–26.

3. Robert Kegan, *In Over Our Heads: The Mental Demands of Modern Life* (Cambridge, MA: Harvard University Press, 1998).

4. Robert Kegan and Lisa Laskow Lahey, *Immunity to Change: How to Overcome It and Unlock the Potential in Yourself and Your Organization* (Boston, MA: Harvard Business School, 2009).

5. Aaron is describing a shift from teacher-directed inquiry to student-directed inquiry. Strategies for making this shift are further explored in John F. Barell, *Problem-Based Learning: An Inquiry Approach,* 2nd ed. (Thousand Oaks, CA: Corwin Press, 2007).

6. Parker J. Palmer, *The Courage to Teach: Exploring the Inner Landscape of a Teacher's Life* (San Francisco: Jossey-Bass, 1998).

CHAPTER 4

Opening the Heart: Enhancing Relationships

1. See for example Mark Youngblood, *Life at the Edge of Chaos: Creating the Quantum Organization* (Dallas: Perceval, 1997).

2. See for example David Bohm, *On Dialogue* (London and New York: Routledge, 1996).

CHAPTER 5

Empowering the Soul: Developing Yourself

1. Parker J. Palmer, *The Courage to Teach: Exploring the Inner Landscape of a Teacher's Life* (San Francisco: Jossey-Bass, 1998), 36.

2. Gretchen M. Spreitzer, "Psychological Empowerment in the Workplace: Dimensions, Measurement, and Validation," *Academy of Management Journal* 38, no. 5 (1995): 1442–65.

3. Ibid.

4. The competence dimension is synonymous with Albert Bandura's notion of self-efficacy (i.e., the belief in one's ability to achieve goals or complete a task effectively). For more information see Albert Bandura, "Self-Efficacy: Toward a Universal Theory of Behavioral Change," *Psychological Review* 8, no. 2 (1977): 191–215.

5. Spreitzer, "Psychological Empowerment in the Workplace."

6. Jay R. Dee, Alan B. Henkin, and Lee Duemer, "Structural Antecedents and Psychological Correlates of Teacher Empowerment," *Journal of Educational Administration* 41, no. 3 (2003): 257–77.

7. Gretchen M. Spreitzer, Mark A. Kizilos, and Stephen W. Nason, "A Dimensional Analysis of the Relationship between Psychological Empowerment and Effectiveness, Satisfaction, and Strain," *Journal of Management* 23, no. 5 (1997): 679–704.

8. Robert E. Quinn, Gretchen M. Spreitzer, and Matthew Brown, "Changing Others through Changing Ourselves: The Transformation of Human Systems," *Journal of Management Inquiry* 9, no. 2 (2000): 147–64.

9. Gretchen M. Spreitzer, Suzanne De Janesz, and Robert E. Quinn, Empowered to Lead: The Role of Psychological Empowerment in Leadership," *Journal of Organizational Behavior* 20, no. 4 (1999): 511–26.

10. For a discussion of job crafting, see Amy Wrzesniewski and Jane E. Dutton, "Crafting a Job: Revisioning Employees as Active Crafters of Their Work," *Academy of Management Review* 26, no. 2 (2001): 179–201.

11. Spreitzer, "Psychological Empowerment in the Workplace."

12. Robert E. Quinn and Gretchen M. Spreitzer, "Entering the Fundamental State of Leadership: A Framework for the Positive Transformation of Self and Others," in *Inspiring Leaders,* ed. Ronald J. Burke and Cary L. Cooper (London and New York: Routledge, 2006), 67–83.

13. Robert E. Quinn, *Building the Bridge as You Walk on It: A Guide for Leading Change* (San Francisco: Jossey-Bass, 2004).

14. Joseph Campbell, *The Hero with a Thousand Faces,* 3rd ed. (New York: New World Library, 2008).

CHAPTER 6

Empowering Others: Teaching That Transforms

1. The idea of transformational teaching is similar to the constructivist approach to teaching and learning. One crucial assumption of the constructivist perspective is that the learner needs to be supported to have ownership of the learning. To learn more see Mustafa Cakir, "Constructivist Approaches to Learning in Science and Their Implications for Science Pedagogy: A Literature Review," *International Journal of Environmental & Science Education* 3, no. 4 (2008): 193–206.

2. Bernard M. Bass, "From Transactional to Transformational Leadership: Learning to Share the Vision," *Organizational Dynamics* (Winter 1990): 19–31.

3. Gary Yukl, *Leadership in Organizations* (Boston, MA: Pearson Education, 2013), 300–27.

4. For example see Paul Tough, *How Children Succeed: Grit, Curiosity, and the Hidden Power of Character* (New York: Houghton Mifflin Harcourt, 2012). See also Carol S. Dweck, *Self-Theories: Their Role in Motivation, Personality, and Development* (Philadelphia: Psychology Press, 2000).

CHAPTER 7

A Process for Development: Embedding Self-Reflection

1. Bruce J. Avolio, Jakari Griffith, Tara S. Wernsing, and Fred O. Walumbwa, "What Is Authentic Leadership Development?" in *Oxford Handbook of*

Positive Psychology and Work, eds. P. Alex Linley, Susan Harrington, and Nicola Garcea (Oxford, England: Oxford University Press, 2010), 39–51.

2. Mary Ann Wolf, *Innovate to Educate: System [Re]Design for Personalized Learning; A Report from the 2010 Symposium* (Washington, DC: Software & Information Industry Association in collaboration with ASCD and the Council of Chief State School Officers, 2010), http://siia.net/pli/presenta tions/perlearnpaper.pdf (accessed January 25, 2014).

3. Daniel Pink, *Drive: The Surprising Truth about What Motivates Us* (New York: Riverhead Books, 2009).

4. Mike Thomas and Katherine Heynoski, *Powerful Practices in the Classroom: Applying Lessons from Highly Effective Teachers to Adopt an Integrated Approach to Professional Development* (Columbus, OH: Battelle for Kids, 2013).

5. Edgar H. Schein, *Organizational Culture and Leadership* (San Francisco: Jossey-Bass, 1985).

6. Robert Kegan and Lisa Laskow Lahey, *How the Way We Talk Can Change the Way We Work: Seven Languages for Transformation* (San Francisco: Jossey-Bass, 2001).

RESOURCE B

Organizational Culture Assessment Instrument for Classrooms

1. The OCAI-C is adapted with permission from the Organizational Culture Assessment Instrument. For details see Kim S. Cameron and Robert E. Quinn, *Diagnosing and Changing Organizational Culture: Based on the Competing Values Framework* (San Francisco: Jossey-Bass, 2006).

Glossary

adaptive confidence　A person's capacity to confidently enter into a new or strange context and to effectively learn one's way toward effectiveness.

adaptive learning system　A system with the capacity to respond and adapt to feedback.

appreciative inquiry　Using questioning to focus people on the most positive aspects of a system.

BFK•Connect Framework　An adaptation of the Competing Values Framework that was derived from long-term interactions with highly effective teachers. Also called the *Connect Framework*.

calling　An instance in which people's vocation is also their avocation. It reflects intrinsic motivation or a strong positive fit between one's values and the work one does.

co-creative perspective of teaching　An orientation that views learning as an emergent process that builds on the relationships between teachers and students. It can include and transcend the more common directive perspective.

collaborative learning　Learning in which more than one person contributes to the knowledge that is used and/or created. Each member of the collaboration is both a teacher and a learner.

collective learning　Learning that is both collaborative and produces shared understanding. The whole group becomes more knowledgeable.

Competing Values Framework　A framework that describes four different and often competing perspectives on effectiveness. It was derived from a study of how organizational scholars describe effectiveness.

continuous improvement   An ongoing process in which one takes action, remains open to feedback, and learns from those actions and then takes new action based on that learning.

culture of inquiry   A group with values that give rise to exploration.

deep change   A shift in personal or collective perspectives that leads to new understanding and new behavior.

developmental change   Movement to higher levels of awareness.

differentiating and integrating   Separating or distinguishing one thing from another (differentiation) and then reconnecting those things into a larger and more comprehensive whole (integration).

directive perspective of teaching   An orientation toward teaching that is hierarchical in character. In this perspective teacher and student are separate roles. The expert teacher transfers knowledge to the student.

either/or thinking   A tendency to see choices or concepts as mutually exclusive alternatives. This reflects a preference for differentiation over integration.

emergent learning   A form of discovery that can occur when one engages a new situation with an open and inquisitive mind. This type of learning typically unfolds during social interactions.

experiential learning   Discovery that is derived from concrete action.

facilitator/facilitative role   A person who acts as a catalyst of collective learning. In this role the teacher both challenges and supports students.

generative learning   Learning that leads to more learning.

highly effective teacher (HET)   Highly effective teachers in the context of this book are teachers who produce significantly more than expected academic growth over multiple years.

idealized influence   A form of moral power associated with transformational leadership. This behavior is an enactment of values that attract and enlist others in a particular enterprise.

incremental change   Learning and change that occurs within an already established set of assumptions.

inspirational motivation   One kind of behavior that is associated with transformational leadership. The articulation of a vision that has the capacity to attract and enlist others in a particular enterprise.

internally directed   The capacity to act authentically out of your own values.

intrinsic motivation   The desire to act in ways that align with your own values.

lead learner   A teacher in a professional learning team who models collaborative learning and continuous improvement.

learning-centered practice   Practice that is characterized by a focus on the process of acquiring knowledge.

life jolt   An experience that compels an individual to rethink and reframe how one lives his or her life.

living beast   A term coined by one teacher in our study that describes the holistic process of learning that occurs when learning becomes fully co-creative. A heightened state of collective learning.

moral power   Power that is derived from one's capacity to present a clear, coherent, and compelling sense of self and life purpose.

outlier   With respect to people, one whose performance is outside the normal or expected range.

paradoxical thinking   The capacity to connect two concepts that are typically regarded as mutually exclusive alternatives. Paradoxical thinking is one way to tie together and integrate opposing ideas.

personalized learning   An approach to learning in which the learning targets, methods, and pace are tailored to the abilities, interests, and needs of individual students.

positive organizations   Systems that are performing at a high level with a culture that invites people to flourish in their work.

powerful practice   A practice that continuously integrates all four quadrants of the Connect Framework.

professional confidence   The capacity to do everything that is necessary to fulfill a job description.

professional learning team (PLT)   A team of teachers who gather on a regular basis to examine their work and learn from one another.

real-time learning   The capacity to learn in the course of pursuing some enterprise.

self-efficacy   A personal sense of being effective in one's work.

self-empowerment   The capacity to creates one's own sense of purpose and then do the necessary work to achieve that purpose.

self-organization   A kind of organization that emerges in response to the work that is being performed.

shared mind   A collective sense of purpose and how that purpose is to be pursued.

slow death   The loss of human energy at the personal or collective level.

small wins   Minor successes that may build confidence in the possibility of achieving larger successes.

stance toward error   Error in any task can be viewed as a step backward or forward. If error is viewed in terms of learning, it helps feed new learning and a sense of progress.

student-centered practice   Practice that is characterized by a focus on students' needs. At the heart of this kind of practice is the question *What's best for kids?*

teacher-centered practice   Practice that is characterized by a focus on instructional methods and the teachers' needs.

transformational influence   The capacity to understand and bring out the best in others.

transformational leadership   The capacity to engage others in a purpose that is larger than themselves. In pursuing this purpose, the system and the people are transformed.

transformational teaching   The capacity to help students challenge their own assumptions, empower themselves, and enact their best selves.

transformative learning   A kind of learning that moves individuals toward a new understanding of self and context and enables the emergence of new capacities.

value-added score   A statistical estimate of the influence that a teacher, school, or school district has on the academic growth of students.

view of group membership   One's understanding of what it means to be part of a group.

Acknowledgments

W E WERE INSPIRED BY THE TEACHER-INTERVIEWEES WHO SO generously shared their stories with us. We continue to be inspired and elevated by you. We wish we were students in your classrooms. We also thank the many teachers in our workshops over the past seven years, who helped us see what positively deviant teaching is all about.

We thank the staff at Battelle for Kids for their extraordinary support throughout the research and writing process. In particular, Executive Director Jim Mahoney was a stalwart of support throughout the project, challenging us to write a book that would have an impact. Julianne Nichols and her marketing team, along with Maggie Malloy who designed the illustrations, were extraordinary in helping us craft a book that would appeal to teachers young and old. Thanks also to Barb Leeper for continuing to find the funds to support the early workshops and research.

We would also like to thank Mary Peters for her early work in identifying HETs and helping facilitate early workshops, as well as Jill Lynch, who did the initial qualitative research that grounded this work.

We would like to thank those who helped fund the work along the way, including the Houston Independent School District, the Tennessee Department of Education, the Ohio Department of Education, the Lubbock Independent School District, and the Gates Foundation.

We thank the faculty and the staff of the Center for Positive Organizations at the Ross School of Business for their support on this book project. We thank Kim Cameron for allowing us to adapt the Organizational Culture Assessment Instrument for classroom purposes. We also thank Managing Director Chris White for his exemplary leadership that freed Bob and Gretchen as co-directors of the center so that they could create space for this writing project.

We thank the leadership and the staff at Berrett-Koehler, who were a joy to work with. Steve Piersanti leads by example; he has created an organization that models positive organizing. Jeevan Sivasubramaniam encouraged and supported us each step of the way. Thank you to them and the many others on the editorial and marketing teams who shared their expertise on how to write for impact!

This book has gone through numerous revisions. We have greatly benefited from the thoughtful comments provided by those who read our earlier drafts, including Barb Cockroft, Lee Collett, Whitney Eubanks, Jim Evers, M. L. Johnson, Gail Kist-Kline, Anna Leinberger, Alexis Martina, Shereeza Mohammed, Kristin Mulrooney, Richard Osguthorpe, Alane Starko, Diane Stultz, Melanie Wightman, and Alan Wilkins. In addition, we appreciate the unfiltered feedback shared by the HETs who are featured in each chapter as we tried to write their stories.

Last but not least, we thank our families for their understanding and love as we pushed through deadlines. We especially thank our spouses, Delsa Quinn, Joe Heynoski, Lu Anne Thomas, and Bob Schoeni, for being there to listen and encourage.

On a final note, we appreciate the amazing experience it was to work with one another. We learned so much as we challenged each other at every step of the way. Who would have believed that a Buckeye and three Wolverines could work so well together?

Index

accountability
    freedom versus, 80–82
    self-empowerment and, 101
    top-down, disempowerment by, 110

achievement, as goal of high-expectations quadrant, 39

action, moving from awareness to, 147–148

adaptive competence, 103–105

Alda, Alan, 49

alienation, as risk with high-expectations quadrant, 39

appreciative interview protocol, 186–187

assumptions
    challenging, 52–53
    opening the mind and. *See* deep change

attractive power, empowerment and, 127–130

authenticity
    to make material relevant, 67
    self-empowerment and, 108–113

autonomy
    empowerment of others and, 137–139
    self-empowerment and, 98, 108–113
    within system, 110–111

awareness, moving to action from, 147–148

becoming a highly effective teacher, 9–26
    deep change and, 12–15
    impetus for, 11–12
    interconnecting perspectives and, 20–23
    learning to become highly effective and, 149–150
    perspectives on teaching and, 16–20
    teacher development and, 23–24
    transformational influence and, 16

Benedict, Ruth, 42

BFK•Connect Framework, 6, 28, 146–147, 152–158, 169–170
    connecting quadrants of, 40–43
    continuous improvement (green) quadrant of. *See* continuous improvement quadrant
    development of, 35
    high-expectations (blue) quadrant of. *See* high-expectations quadrant
    home quadrant of, 40–41
    relationships (yellow) quadrant of. *See* relationships quadrant
    stable environment (red) quadrant of. *See* stable environment quadrant

About the Authors

Shauri Quinn Dewey

Robert E. Quinn

Robert E. Quinn holds the Margaret Elliot Tracey Collegiate Professorship at the University of Michigan and serves on the faculty of Organization and Management at the Ross Business School. He is one of the co-founders and the current faculty co-director of the Center for Positive Organizations. Quinn's research and teaching interests focus on leadership, organizational change, and effectiveness. He has published 16 books on these subjects. He is particularly known for his work on the Competing Values Framework. He has 30 years of experience consulting with major corporations and government agencies.

Matt Reese

Katherine Heynoski

Katherine Heynoski is a powerful practices senior specialist at Battelle for Kids. Building on her research with highly effective teachers and principals, she conducts training and develops tools and resources to support educators' professional growth. At the heart of her work as a researcher and a practitioner is a desire to help individuals, teams, and organizations continuously improve their practice. Prior to joining Battelle for Kids, Katherine worked as an instructor and a research assistant while completing her PhD at the University of Michigan. She has also worked as a Lean Six Sigma Black Belt for General Electric.

Katherine has published in *Organizational Dynamics* and *Research in Organizational Change and Development*. She also serves on the board of the Organization Development and Change Division of the Academy of Management. She lives in Dublin, Ohio, with her husband and two daughters.

Mike Thomas

Mike Ericson

Mike Thomas has worked for the past 11 years at Battelle for Kids to improve the quality of teaching and learning in schools across the country. As a senior director of innovation, he has designed tools and delivered professional development to build the capacity of teachers and administrators. Much of this work has focused on the diagnostic and school improvement uses of value-added data. He recently co-authored the book *How to Use Value-Added Analysis to Improve Student Learning.* Over the past seven years, Mike has conducted workshops and assembled focus groups of high value-added teachers and principals to better understand what constitutes effective practice. This book is the culmination of that work.

Prior to joining Battelle for Kids, Mike served as the director of the Central Ohio Principals' Academy and the co-coordinator of the pre-service elementary and middle school Masters of Education program at The Ohio State University. In this role he received a Distinguished Teaching Award. Mike spent the first 12 years of his career as a middle school math and science teacher.

Mike currently resides in Westerville, Ohio, with his wife, Lu Anne, and their dog, Kali. His daughter Emily is entering her senior year at Ohio State University; his son, Chris, is an officer in the US Air Force; and his daughter Lindsay is a nurse and the mother of his eight-year-old granddaughter, Kameron.

Gretchen M. Spreitzer

Scott Stewart

Gretchen M. Spreitzer is the Keith E. and Valerie J. Alessi Professor of Business Administration at the Ross School of Business at the University of Michigan. She is also the co-director of the Center for Positive Organizations. She joined the Michigan faculty in 2001 after spending nine years on the faculty of the University of Southern California Marshall School of Business. She is passionate about helping people develop as leaders.

Her research focuses on employee empowerment and leadership development, particularly within a context of organizational change. Her most recent research focuses on how organizations can enable people to thrive at work and become their best selves. She has co-authored six books (including another Berrett-Koehler book, titled *How to Be a Positive Leader: Small Action, Big Impact* with Jane Dutton) and many articles on these topics. She teaches leadership and change courses to undergraduate and graduate students and executives at Ross. She has been elected to leadership positions in the Academy of Management and the Western Academy of Management. She lives in Ann Arbor, Michigan, with her husband, who is a public policy economist, and two teenage daughters.

About Battelle for Kids

B ATTELLE FOR KIDS IS A NATIONAL NOT-FOR-PROFIT ORGANIZATION that provides counsel and innovative solutions to today's complex educational improvement challenges. Its mission is *Bringing clarity to school improvement*. Its team of education, business, communications, and technology professionals works collaboratively with school districts, state departments of education, and other education-focused organizations in support of this mission.

We at Battelle for Kids have partnered with educators in nearly 30 states as well as the District of Columbia and Hong Kong to help them navigate the often complex process of turning policy into effective practice in schools. At the heart of this work is an unwavering focus on accelerating student growth. We specialize in developing strategies in the areas that we believe make all the difference:

- Recruiting, developing, and retaining the *right people*
- Identifying and providing them with access to the *right measures*
- Ensuring that they can use that information to effectively implement the *right practices*
- Strategically communicating with and engaging all stakeholders using the *right messages*

Over the past decade, Battelle for Kids has seen student success grow dramatically when educators have access to and the capacity to understand and use value-added information in combination with multiple measures to guide instruction and accelerate student growth. Central to our work is a commitment to identify highly effective teachers through multiple measures, celebrate their achievements, learn from their practices, and share the lessons learned to elevate the performance of all teachers so that all children can achieve their potential.

Battelle for Kids has spent more than six years systematically studying the practices of more than 350 highly effective educators in Ohio, Tennessee, and Texas, who year after year have made extraordinary academic gains with kids. We have conducted hundreds of hours of focus groups and in-depth interviews with these educators from urban, suburban, and rural settings to discover what they do that contributes to student success. Teaching and learning are complex. Our goal in researching highly effective educators is not to simplify but rather to make it easier to understand all the factors that go into being a great teacher.

To help others learn how to increase their effectiveness, we provide high-quality, blended learning experiences developed with educators to increase assessment literacy and the use of formative instruction and summative measures for instructional decision-making. Additionally, Battelle for Kids has developed a suite of professional learning offerings grounded in the Connect Framework. By integrating their practice across the four dimensions of the framework, education professionals can improve their performance:

- *Teachers* can assess their strengths and stretch core instructional practices into more powerful integrated practices.

- *School leaders* can increase their effectiveness to cultivate thriving school environments. We offer academies, workshops, and coaching to support this work.

Applying the Connect Framework systemwide provides a common language and approach that makes implementation and professional learning more impactful—leading to increased effectiveness for all.

Learn more about Battelle for Kids' services and solutions available to accelerate student learning at:

BattelleforKids.org and BFKConnect.org

Connect:

twitter.com/BattelleforKids and facebook.com/battelleforkidsorg

About the Center for Positive Organizations

What Are Positive Organizations?

There are abundant resources hidden within and around your organization—resources like commitment, creativity, inspiration, generosity, integrity, and authentic leadership. Too often these powerful resources are trapped within rigid processes, structures, and systems. These resources, if tapped, can lead to vibrant, energized people contributing at the highest levels in thriving workplaces. These are assets that can generate extraordinary performance, both individually and collectively, at all levels of the organization.

We call those workplaces that have learned to unlock these exceptional human resources *positive organizations.*

What Is the Center for Positive Organizations?

The Center for Positive Organizations is the central place for researchers, students, and leaders seeking to study or build positive organizations.

Our research focuses on such topics as positive leadership, purpose and meaning, ethics and virtues, and relationships and culture in organizations. Our global community of scholars comprises more than 300 academics at many of the world's top research institutions.

We take this research to a wide audience through our educational programs, communications channels, Research in Action tools, and organizational partnerships. Our research has been effectively applied in such companies as Google, McKinsey, and Humana and such universities as Wharton, Harvard Business School, and the Ross School of Business.

The contributions of the Center for Positive Organizations to management science, and to changing management practices, have been recognized by the Academy of Management. Our work appears regularly in academic journals, popular press books, and mainstream media outlets.

What Are Some Ways to Get Involved?

- **Learn more.** Review the aggregated research and blogs on our website (CenterforPos.org)

- **Stay connected.** Follow us on Facebook and Twitter or join our mailing list.

- **Join the community.** Attend our events, such as the Positive Business Conference.

- **Take a deep dive.** Enroll in our programs at undergraduate, graduate, and executive levels.

- **Implement our research in your organization.** Apply our Research in Action tools or explore an organizational partnership.

- **Sponsor or donate.** Support our programs, activities, and events.

Contact Us

The Center for Positive Organizations
Ross School of Business
University of Michigan
positiveorg@umich.edu | http://positiveorgs.bus.umich.edu

Berrett–Koehler
Publishers

Berrett-Koehler is an independent publisher dedicated to an ambitious mission: *Creating a World That Works for All*.

We believe that to truly create a better world, action is needed at all levels—individual, organizational, and societal. At the individual level, our publications help people align their lives with their values and with their aspirations for a better world. At the organizational level, our publications promote progressive leadership and management practices, socially responsible approaches to business, and humane and effective organizations. At the societal level, our publications advance social and economic justice, shared prosperity, sustainability, and new solutions to national and global issues.

A major theme of our publications is "Opening Up New Space." Berrett-Koehler titles challenge conventional thinking, introduce new ideas, and foster positive change. Their common quest is changing the underlying beliefs, mindsets, institutions, and structures that keep generating the same cycles of problems, no matter who our leaders are or what improvement programs we adopt.

We strive to practice what we preach—to operate our publishing company in line with the ideas in our books. At the core of our approach is stewardship, which we define as a deep sense of responsibility to administer the company for the benefit of all of our "stakeholder" groups: authors, customers, employees, investors, service providers, and the communities and environment around us.

We are grateful to the thousands of readers, authors, and other friends of the company who consider themselves to be part of the "BK Community." We hope that you, too, will join us in our mission.

A BK Life Book

This book is part of our BK Life series. BK Life books change people's lives. They help individuals improve their lives in ways that are beneficial for the families, organizations, communities, nations, and world in which they live and work. To find out more, visit **www.bk-life.com**.

Berrett–Koehler
Publishers

A community dedicated to creating
a world that works for all

Dear Reader,

Thank you for picking up this book and joining our worldwide community
of Berrett-Koehler readers. We share ideas that bring positive change into
people's lives, organizations, and society.

To welcome you, we'd like to offer you a free e-book. You can pick from
among twelve of our bestselling books by entering the promotional code
BKP92E here: http://www.bkconnection.com/welcome.

When you claim your free e-book, we'll also send you a copy of our e-news-
letter, the *BK Communiqué*. Although you're free to unsubscribe, there are
many benefits to sticking around. In every issue of our newsletter you'll find

- A free e-book
- Tips from famous authors
- Discounts on spotlight titles
- Hilarious insider publishing news
- A chance to win a prize for answering a riddle

Best of all, our readers tell us, "Your newsletter is the only one I actually
read." So claim your gift today, and please stay in touch!

Sincerely,

Charlotte Ashlock
Steward of the BK Website

Questions? Comments? Contact me at bkcommunity@bkpub.com.